Letters for My Sisters

First published 2014 by Transgress Press

Library of Congress Cataloguing in Publication Data

Letter for My Sisters / edited by Andrea James and Deanne Thornton

Copyright © 2014 Andrea James and Deanne Thornton

ISBN: 1499342039
Transgress Press, Oakland, CA

Letters for My Sisters

Transitional Wisdom in Retrospect

EDITED BY ANDREA JAMES AND DEANNE THORNTON

Hung Jury:

Testimonies of Genital Surgery by Transsexual Men

Edited by Trystan T. Cotten

Letters for My Brothers:

Transitional Wisdom in Retrospect (3rd Edition)

Edited by Megan M. Rohrer and Zander Keig

Manning Up:

Transsexual Men on Finding Brotherhood, Family and Themselves

Edited by Zander Keig and Mitch Kellaway

CONTENTS

ꕥ STRENGTH ꕥ

᭒ HOPE ᭒

Dedication

To those people who find themselves on the wrong side of some gender line. May you find the hope and wisdom you need to be yourselves and to make a better world for all of us.

"For beautiful eyes, look for the good in others; for beautiful lips, speak only words of kindness; and for poise, walk with the knowledge that you are never alone."

— Audrey Hepburn

"Being a strong woman is very important to me. But doing it all on my own is not."

— Reba McIntire

Editors' Foreword

I met Zander and his wife Margaret at a celebration for a mutual friend. After several more meetings and long evenings together, we discovered that we had as much in common as we had differences. He had shared his book *Letters For My Brothers* with me, and this was the germ of an idea that there should be something similar for trans women.

The chance meeting was just the surface of a very deep ocean. Hidden in the depths is a theme, whether conscious or unconscious, of community. The idea to bring a collection of journeymen (journey-women?) together to share their hard-won wisdom with others is an act of community.

This idea is what I hope this work encourages. After we transition, we sometimes hang on to patterns from our experiences in the male world. One of these is a "Lone Ranger" approach to solving problems. We need to leave that behind. Whether through nurture or nature, women are excellent collaborators. Yes, we can band together for a convention, event or protest, but we need to bring this to a personal level. My hope is that you will create a community of your own, and that your community will grow and collaborate with other communities. I hope this small germ of an idea can grow to make the world a hospitable place for everyone who sees their gender as different from what they have been assigned.

My thanks to my "big brother" Zander for all that he has contributed to this project. To my editing partner Andrea for all her guidance in making this happen. To all the trans women that have added words here. To my sisters Tanya, Andrea, Callie, Debra, Lana and Susan for being there when I needed you. To Margaret, for understanding why her husband is out with another woman all those times. To my GG sisters Pennie, Drew, Jameson, Pam, Daryl, Tamara, Cathy, Suzie, Francesca, and Jayne, thanks for inviting me into your community.

Deanne Thornton

Although Dee has been kind enough to list me as her co-editor, this volume was largely produced through her yearlong efforts. I'd like to express my gratitude to her and to all the women who shared their wisdom for this project. I hope you find some insight, comfort, and strength within these pages.

Andrea James

Foreword

L Y N N   C O N W A Y

When I began my own transition in the mid-1960s, I didn't have support groups or websites, or books like this, or any of the other resources so common today. Instead, I had to rely on what little oral tradition there was back then for those wishing to transition, and on letters, hand-written or typed, then stamped and mailed.

One letter I wrote went to Dr. Harry Benjamin, the pioneering physician who helped me live the life I so desperately needed to live. Once we connected, I was able to become the woman I am today, with a successful career, a happy marriage and a deep sense of fulfillment.

I know the power a letter can have in changing your life. Over the years, many trans women's first attempts to reach out came to me in the form of letters or emails. They've often told me how important it was to receive an encouraging reply; how it empowered them to explore and connect further.

The women who wrote this collection of letters are sharing their hard-earned wisdom because they want to help you. They want this to be easier and safer for you. They want you to be happy. Some transitioned long ago; others were in the midst of their own transitions. All of them realize that work created for us and by us can make a huge difference in turning our dreams into realities.

I hope you find voices here that connect with your own thoughts and feelings, and that those voices empower you with strength and hope for the future.

Introduction

ANDREA JAMES AND DEANNE THORNTON

For too long now we have let others define and describe us. Clinicians, academics, and the media have held control over our psychological, medical, and public classifications. No matter how well-meaning, they do not understand us, framing us in their own misunderstandings.

This misunderstanding goes much deeper than just the views of the world. Their definitions of us have influenced what we think of ourselves. In our desperate need to be accepted, we have used their incomplete understanding to describe ourselves to others, with the mistaken idea that these familiar words would open the door to true understanding.

This work excludes the voices of others. The only voices here are our own. The voices are varied and sometimes seem conflicting. They are from different ages and backgrounds. By themselves they are quiet, but brought together they are loud. Their individuality forms a harmony.

This book is not a collection of biographies but a distillation of our thoughts and feelings about who we are, where we have come from and how we got here. Apart from the fact that we have all transitioned, the letters have no common thread. Each of us has shared our own "truth" as honestly as we could. Since there is no chronology, you can read these essays in any order you choose.

Because true harmony requires a structure we have given much thought about how best to form our parts. We have chosen four sections each one marking a major part of transition. We start with the most important, "Acceptance." Look here if you need to decide if transition is for you or when you need confirmation that you are on the right path. Next is "Strength." Here you will find the thoughts and feelings from deep inside the transition process. Then we have "Hope." Transition is a difficult process and we all fail sometimes. Look here for the words of encouragement that we all need from time to time. Finally we have "Gratitude." The noblest of virtues and the proper place a journey of self-discovery should lead.

Intermixed with the essays specifically written for LFMS are contributions sent to the precursor to our book www.tsroadmap.com. These online contributions formed one of the first collaborations to our community and are distinguished by the "TS Roadmap" following the author's name. The authors' names have been changed and any identifying information within these letters was removed by agreement at the time of submission to tsroadmap.com. For these same privacy reasons, these contributions do not have corresponding biographies at the end of this volume.

This work was inspired by a collection for trans men. Both works seek to inspire other collaborative works for other gender outlaws, in our own voices. To regain control of our images and show everyone who we are, we hope you will join us in adding your own voice to our harmony.

Acceptance

"When I let go of what I am, I become what I might be."

— *Lao Tsu*

"Understanding is the first step to acceptance, and only with acceptance can there be recovery."

— *J. K. Rowling*

The Tao of Transition

DEANNE THORNTON

I have something to tell you about what lies ahead of you. It is important stuff, and I know that some of it will be hard for you to hear. Some of it you may not understand at first, and the rest you may have trouble believing. Just stay with me and hold all of the skepticism and sarcasm until after we are finished.

I know that your life is hard right now. It's been hard for a long time. There is something about you that is different. When you try to tell people about it, there just aren't the words. It's hard to explain something to others for which they have no way to imagine. You're not even sure that you understand it, but it is still there. Don't worry, the words will come, and when they come, there will be many of them. The scariest will be "Transsexual." It will take a while for you to accept that this is you, but accepting it is the only way forward. When you are ready, read on.

So you are the "T-word." All that end of the world stuff you feared didn't happen, and you're still here. At this point you will want to tell people, and there are people you need to talk with. Still, you want to be careful at this stage. Not everyone needs to be told, and not everyone whom you tell needs to know everything. When it comes to this, less is more. There will come a time when you will wish that you didn't have to tell anyone.

Your world is going to change. Some of those changes you are going to like. Some you will not. As with other things in your life, you will not always have control over which changes you get. With the parts you can control you need to make good decisions. You are going to make mistakes. When you do, it won't be the end of the world. There are people who can help you. They have been where you are and have made some of the same mistakes. Seek them out and listen to them. Avoid people that want to tell you how to do things that they haven't done themselves. No guru or mentor can lead you to a skill they don't possess. Beware of people who offer to help you for a fee. Not that you shouldn't pay professionals who provide a useful service. Just be sure that it's what you want and they don't exploit you because you are in transition. Many people who I thought were fair and helpful at the time turned out to be a waste of money. The rule here would be to seek out recommendations from those of who have had a chance to reflect on their own transition experiences.

People will start to notice you are different. They will begin to treat you differently. It's exciting when people begin recognizing the parts of you that have been hidden for so long. We all need validation, particularly when you are risking so much. At times, others will notice changes that you aren't aware of or might not notice changes that you believe are monumental. This is like being on a roller coaster and it will be hard to not become disappointed with the reactions of the denser part of the population. Take the positive validations and consider what caring people tell you, but you don't have to change something because others think you should. It's your life and you are the only one who can give meaning and purpose to it.

It is best that you keep an open mind. As your place in the world changes, the way you see the world will have to change with it. The alternative is to become the same old person you were in your different body, and you don't want that. These changes will be the least noticeable to everyone else and the hardest for you. They will cause you to rethink many of the things you held as true. This can be the scariest part of all. At times it will feel like you no longer have solid ground beneath your feet and your insides are filled with Jello. Try to let acceptance replace that fear. Let a sense of wonder be your guide. Eventually you will find confidence in uncertainty and strength in humility. This is where you will build the real you, the one that has been there all along.

There are going to be some people who will not like what you are doing. They will not want to be around you anymore. They may even prevent you from getting a place to live or a job that you need. You may be able to change some of them, but not all of them. You can't let them stop you. You've made it this far without them; you can make it the rest of the way. The best way for you to fight them is to succeed. The more successful you become, the less they can complain.

When you were a child and considering your future career you might have said things like astronaut, president, doctor, or even a something as ridiculous as a character from your favorite cartoon. While those desires were real at the time they were formed from a child's view of the world. Something similar is happing to you now. You have a man's view of what constitutes a woman. As you plan what you become I hope that you consider that what you envision as an ideal woman may not be the ideal later. There are many types of women in this world but you only have to be the one that really fits you. Remember true beauty comes from confidence and compassion not the Barbie dream house.

Just like the perfect dress needs the right shoes and purse, you are going to need a new life to go along with all these changes. You don't have to decide what that will be right away. Give yourself time to find out who you are. Then you will know where you are going and who will come along with you. What you want right now may not be what you want tomorrow. Even tomorrow's desires may be different in a week, month, or year. None of this means that you will have the life of your dreams, but you can have a life that is yours.

Now this is the end game stuff. If you are not ready for it, then stop reading here and pick this up when you are in the right place and time.

So you've made it all this way. You are a new person, with a life that may not be perfect, but it's still your own. Now comes the really big secret. Transition doesn't end. That's right. It goes on and on. There will be milestones and goals that will be reached and periods that can be marked by significant events. But the journey continues. As long as you breathe, as long as your heart beats, you will still be changing. Your thoughts, beliefs and aspirations will morph. Who you are will change along with them. The people in your life will change, some relationships will grow deeper and others will grow apart. Keep your eyes on the goal and not on the past. If you do, one day you'll discover that you have reached the point where who you once were is now the dream and who you are is the reality.

In all of this you need to see just one thing; the beauty of being your-self—your true self. No New Age philosophy here, just a realization that you spent a portion of your life living as something and someone you were not. All you have done is strip away everything that wasn't you. What is left is a purity, a comfort with yourself and feeling of being natural. With all that comes a new level of vulnerability. This is not something to fear, it's all a part of being a woman. That is what you have always been, what you will always be.

Exhibit Closed until Further Notice
(When the Sideshow Attraction Turns Out to Be You)

DEVON
(FROM THE TS ROADMAP)

L ooking back at it now from a vantage point 12 years later, my transition was a nightmare. Not that I thought it was smooth sailing at the time, but I couldn't really appreciate the magnitude of the ordeal while I was smack in the middle of it. It took a while for it to sink in—about a decade, in fact. Optimist that I was then, I had expected any problems to be minor. I was lucky enough to be passable from the get-go and completely accepted as female in public, so that wasn't a problem. No, most of the trouble stemmed from a single source—my friends.

For someone planning eventually to live stealth, I made several mistakes when I transitioned, and they were lulus. The first was remaining in the same place, the second was maintaining contact with people I knew before, and the last—a really egregious one—was allowing friends to exploit me unmercifully. Certainly, these blunders are understandable—this was new territory, and I didn't know any better. But that doesn't stop me from digging my nails into my palms when I recall that period of time.

When a person transitions, he or she is typically extremely vulnerable, hungry for acceptance and approval, and I was no different. I'd lost a few friends and some family over this, and I desperately craved support. To my joy, my remaining friends heaped loads of reassurance and validation on me. They seemed so enthusiastic and pleased to be a part of my transition. It felt wonderful to be surrounded by all that acceptance, I can't deny it. At the time it was mother's milk.

I was inundated by dinner and party invitations, people wanted me to go places and do things with them, folks called or dropped over just to hang out with me. I was flabbergasted by all the unexpected attention. One married couple in particular took me under their wing. I had known the guy for a number of years, but then his wife and I became quite close, best girlfriends. They introduced me to new people, all of whom seemed anxious to meet me. In fact, between them and the rest of my friends I was meeting a lot of new people.

Soon, I began feeling uneasy about the number of people who knew about my situation. There were some troubling signs that had escaped my attention previously. Many of my new friends seemed to be titillated. It was evident in their excited expressions, in the way their eyes glistened, and in how the talk centered around transsexual topics. They couldn't get enough. Belatedly, I woke up to what was happening. For many of them, I was an unwitting guest on their personal "Jerry Springer Show." For others, I became an opportunity for them to demonstrate how admirably open-minded they were.

Regardless of their motivations, all the elation and exuberance I'd felt about receiving so much acceptance dissipated quickly. I felt used. Through sheer naivety and gullibility, I'd allowed the situation to get completely out of control. It was my own fault, and I owned it. Nevertheless, I resented the insensitivity of my so-called "friends" in taking advantage of me at a time when I was most vulnerable.

Unfortunately, by this point, although I was unaware of the extent of it, my friends had informed so many people about me—people who, in turn, told other people, who told still other people, and so on—that the circle of insiders with knowledge about my situation had grown exponentially. After so many iterations of gossip mongering, it was only a matter of time before things started turning sour in a big way. Weirdoes began coming out of the woodwork.

The first one to enter the picture was an ex-con who called me "li'l darlin'" when he introduced himself at a party. This heavily tattooed character expressed great interest, grinning at me with very large, very white teeth. He told me that he had known some "she-males" in the joint, and really dug them, so he figured I might like to spend some time with a righteous dude like him. I informed Captain Mullet that I wasn't interested.

Next, the "Six Degrees of Separation" principle came into play. Unbeknownst to me, a neighbor who lived in the duplex across the street, a husky guy with a beard whom I'd never spoken to, had found out about me through a mutual acquaintance. I started getting harassing phone calls from him, although I didn't know he was the culprit at first. In a low voice, he would mutter veiled threats, things like "I know who you really are, and you're not going to get away with it." Unfortunately, he had CallerID blocking, so at the phone company's suggestion I used *57 (Last Call Record) to record his number at the central office; I also started tape recording his calls. After three more, the police identified him as my neighbor and paid him a visit. One of the cops told me the guy's story was that he was "just joking around," and he'd promised not to do it again. I was relieved when he moved shortly afterward.

Finally, there was the attorney I met who turned out to be a "transfan." Introduced by a friend-of-a-friend, he confided that he was looking for a relationship with someone with "both male and female qualities." He found me "an exotic creature." I told this scumbag to tell his story walking.

I'd had enough. Clearly, drastic action was required to rectify things. I could see no other option but to get the hell out of Dodge. I relocated, and in so doing, cut off contact with the entire group of people who'd exploited me so ruthlessly. I left no forwarding address or phone number. By all appearances, I'd dropped off the face of the earth. The speculation was that I'd taken a job with a company on the East Coast. No doubt quite a few people were sorely disappointed to lose their private sideshow exhibit.

Since then I've lived a life of relative stealth. No one knows of my situation—not my employer, associates at work, friends, or the guys I date. However, although distance separates my former friends and me I'm always aware of the possibility of worlds colliding. It hangs over my head like the Sword of Damocles, the price I pay for my carelessness. Still, I was incredibly lucky, luckier than I had any right to expect. I managed to escape a dangerous situation relatively unscathed—sadder, but infinitely wiser.

Perhaps my unfortunate experience can provide a lesson for others. After you transition, if people seem to descend upon you in droves, offering friendship and approval, watch out. Be on guard. Be wary of overly friendly types. Turn down invitations. Don't roll out the welcome mat. You do not want to meet lots of new people during this time. Granted, all that attention is very intoxicating, but you'll be better off without it. Here's a news flash: People are not tripping over themselves to meet you just because of your sparkling personality. Most importantly, make it clear to everyone you know that you expect them to protect your privacy, which means keeping their mouths shut about your situation. Try to make them understand that loose lips could place you in grave danger. Heed this advice. Learn from my mistakes.

Otherwise, a tattooed, mullet-wearing ex-con with a shirt unbuttoned down to his navel might soon be paying you a visit, li'l darlin'.

Hello Beautiful

SHEVON PROPST

Hello Beautiful,

I know you don't think you are right now, but trust me; you are more amazing than you'll ever know! You will do some things in this life that you can't even imagine yet. You will love so intensely you'll be in pieces, you'll cry for good and for bad, you'll laugh so hard you'll have tears in your eyes. You'll see babies being born and old friends and loved ones join the ancestors. But most importantly you will eventually look back and smile. You will be so proud of yourself that your heart will swell up and you won't be able to contain yourself. It will be worth all the stress you're feeling right now about the transition and about your body. How you want to look and present yourself to the world all takes time.

The most important thing you can do for yourself right now is to trust your heart and know who you are inside. Ask yourself—at my core do I know for sure without any doubt that I want to live my life as the woman I am? If your heart says yes, then trust it and follow its dream. I promise you, it won't betray you. When you come out, do so with dignity, intelligence and wit. Remember this is about you, not about how other people see you. It's also not about how other people want you to be. Always remember we place an expectation on people in our lives, we expect them to be a certain thing or to do certain things. But that's not compassion and that's not love. When you can let go of what others think you should be, or what they think you should do, then you are entrusting your heart to follow the path that you came to this planet to walk.

You will make a huge difference in others' lives as you live the way you choose to. You will pave roads that others will walk on. You will change hearts and minds. You will lead others, even if in silence. Always know you will never truly see the difference that you will make in this world, but trust me, you will make a huge impact on others.

Two more things before I close this letter. Be nice to the boys; yes, you can wrap them around your fingers and make them do your bidding, but be nice. One day there will be an amazing boy who will smile at you from ear to ear, he will grab your heart and make you crazy in love. Be nice to him, he's worth keeping. Second thing, hormones! Take it easy on them, the more you take will not make your boobies bigger faster! Listen to a good doctor who has treated other Transwomen and stick to that plan. And if you feel grumpy and mean, don't take it out on anyone. My mom always said "every woman has a period, that's not an excuse to be a bitch."

Lots of love,
Your sister,
Shevon Propst

Mid 20's Observations

KAY
(FROM THE TS ROADMAP)

Hiyas! I thought I'd share a lil' bit of my experience with you. I started transitioning just before my 26th birthday (do I still qualify as a young TS then?), and only in the last six to eight months have had any success in passing, as I plan to go stealth, which is my main goal. I also liked what you said about the attractive ones not being better, just lucky. I think that's something I needed to hear, to be honest with you. I'm petrified of giving off this air that I'm better than anyone, especially those who don't pass well.

Presenting as female now, I have issues with society. I don't really mind getting looked at, although getting honked at bothers me, and a guy stopping his car to ask if I need a ride is just really REALLY creepy!! Which seems to be my main problem in adjusting to the female role; a lot of people seem to think I'm attractive, which is nice, although I don't see myself as such. But the problems that can cause can be really bad for someone who wasn't raised as a female and is not used to the attention that being perceived as attractive can bring.

You take someone who was raised male, and is used to more or less being looked over (and listened to quite a bit, I should add) rather than looked at. I was pretty much taken as another male electronic musician by society at large most of my life. When I was trying to build up a career doing music, I was thought of as just another geekboi with a computer and a guitar. You take someone who is used to socializing like that and being listened to, put them in a situation where they draw attention based on the way people feel they look, and life becomes DRASTICALLY different, and not all of the changes are for the best.

Hardly anyone except my close friends and family really seem to take me seriously anymore, since I have lost whatever male privilege I had. Straight men around me tend to stare at certain parts of my anatomy. I now understand the phrase "My eyes are up here" all too well. With most guys (and even some lesbians), it can be hard to communicate. Sometimes I have to repeat myself or interrupt a lot to even get what I'm trying to say listened to in the first place. Other TS's seem to have a hard time giving support to me because (as one of my TS activist friends said) I haven't been "raked over the coals enough"; i.e. I don't have a marriage or kids to worry about. That may be true, but, as is the case with most TS's, I have lost the majority of my family on both sides, and quite a few friends I had in my prior life, to the whole issue of my transitioning.

The upside, though, is that I also have moments where, even just going out shopping or something, women call me "ma'am" and make small talk with me. More NORMAL moments in life, in my honest opinion. That didn't really happen prior to my transitioning. Most of my life, I hadn't felt any sort of emotional connection with either gender. Guys just scared me, and I didn't understand why they acted the way they did, while women didn't really make an attempt to socialize with me as much because I was male. So having the small talk is a good thing.

Also my friendships have changed drastically. Those friends that saw the guy me have stopped talking to me completely, which kinda proves to me the type of friends they were.

The friends I've made since I started transitioning have always seen me as Kay and nothing else, so it's easy for them to treat me as female. My friendships with other women also have this underlying current of understanding that I didn't feel with either gender in my prior life. There's more of a sense of knowing where other women are coming from, as well as just knowing what dealing with guys are like from the women's point of view. I can say that, even with the drawback of now being seen as an object or just tits and ass, the positive out-weighs the negative aspects by a mile!

Well, that's my experience so far. Currently, I'm back doing music, and my gender now seems to be a plus insofar as gaining fans. There aren't many women doing electronic music, and it seems that it makes people curious about what my music sounds like (for some reason, they think it's going to be something drastically different or something! LOL)

Anyways, any feedback you could give is more than welcome. And thank you for having the site up. A lot of girls like us need support, and it's good to have an understanding person there to talk to.

Ciao!
Kay

Fear No More

LARA LANDIS

Dear Shawn,

Our youth has been confusing. I know about the isolation and ostracism we face, and I also know that our stubborn attitude will help you get through it. This is not a pleasant time for you, and I'm not about to tell you things will get better. The future has many unpleasant surprises in store.

I have not introduced myself yet, but Lara Landis is my name. I am the you that exists some twenty years from now. We got past the time when we cried ourselves to sleep almost every night. We also stopped asking the universe why we were singled out for such abuse from our peers. We also prayed to become female every night. As it so often happens, these prayers will be answered, but not as we hoped.

Let us discuss the fears of our youth. We shy away from people because we think telling others we are female will cause us more grief. While we both know that people can be cruel, most people are not as cruel as we suspect. The social environment we faced in our school years is one that we will never face again. In fact, the bullies we knew in high school, we won't meet again. Two of the worst tormentors will end up in jail. When we finally do come out as a woman, we will find that our imagination has put us through scenarios that are worse than what happens to us in real life. Not everyone will accept this change, and our father is the person who has the hardest time accepting our transition. We expected this, so do not be surprised.

We both know we will keep this secret, much to our detriment. Once we fully accept who we are, we find that much of our anxiety subsides. One regret remains. We both wish we had not taken so much time to realize this. It held us back, but let us return to the problems of our youth.

Our family knows that deeper issues exist, even if we do not yet know. We are depressed, and we suffer from social anxiety disorder. A brief and unsuccessful attempt at a naval career helps us realize that we have these problems, even though we do not immediately begin treatment. Eventually, anti-depressants will help us maintain our mood, but one dark period begins several years after. It begins when our mother's mental health severely declines. A year after her death, we try to overdose on pills. Life continues to batter us after this, but we are tougher emotionally than we give ourselves credit for being.

We will hang in there. Even though we make many mistakes, the Hell we faced in our youth eventually ends. Even though the information found in this epistle seems depressing, all is not lost. Our Mormon background has helped us understand that there are times when we must endure. Not all is bleak for us, however. Blogs and the World Wide Web—words we do not know yet—will give us the opportunity to earn money writing. We will also become a reporter focusing on asexual issues, but we earn little to no money from this. Oh, we do identify as asexual for several years, but when we start hormone replacement therapy, we become less sure of this label. In the past, we believed that we were attracted to women simply because that is what society expected.

We write this from Terre Haute, an Indiana city. We both find this to be an unlikely event, but it does happen. When we do start on this process, we will find we have new sisters. Be sure to tell them that sometime.

Lara Landis

When I Was Born

JANIS BOOTH

When I was born, I lacked the gift of language. I knew who I was but was unable to tell anyone. This doctor person looked at my body and diagnosed me as male, then he slapped my behind. Not a very nice way to be greeted into the world. First he screwed up on who I was, and then he hit me for no reason.

My mom and dad took me home. They fed me, clothed me, cared for me, and gave me hugs and love. I needed them to survive and I knew it. It was easy to tell what made them smile and what made them frown, so I did the things that made them smile even when I really did not want to.

I quickly learned what the big people liked. When I was hungry, they would help me, so I did the things that made them happy and I did the things that I thought would get smiles and hugs. I avoided those things that made them react with frowns, even though some of those things were what I really wanted to do. The longer I acted in concert with the smiles of the big people, the more the big people approved.

I grew older and I had some confusion. I knew how to behave to please the big people but it was not how I wanted to behave. On those few occasions that I behaved naturally, I received frowns and corrections. I didn't like the frowns, and I hated the corrections. I wasn't stupid, so I learned quickly how to act to get the smiles and acted that way.

I absorbed a set of rules on how to behave and what my life goals should be. The goals I learned were not the same as the drive I felt inside, but I needed those big people so I had to please them. I had to keep them smiling.

When I finally reached an age where my dependence on the big people was lessening, my internal compass had already been set. I had learned that there were things I was supposed to like and goals I was supposed to strive for; I learned that the ones I felt inside were not OK and needed to be hidden lest I get frowns and disapproval. No one forced me to be that way. No one had an agenda for me. The big people had believed that silly doctor and I was unable to correct them. Now it was too late.

I lived my life that way for sixty years. I met many of the goals I had accepted. I even met some of my own goals. I had some good times and some success, but there was always something missing. I was never able to experience happiness fully.

Then, suddenly, one day the real me exploded and refused to hide any longer. I wrestled with guilt over having lied to everyone all my life about who I am. Then it occurred to me that all I had really done was comply with the wishes of those around me.

Today I have stopped suppressing my own wishes. I have stopped hiding who I really am to please those around me. I have let go of my shame for who I am. I am fully here and living my life honestly. No more rules given to me by others, I live by my own rules. I know what it feels like to be happy.

No Matter Where I Go

CHERYL MILLER

The first part of the newspaper that I read every day is the comic section. I do it because I like to start the day with a smile before I get into all the negativity the paper has to offer. Usually I get a little chuckle, and every so often I pick up some words of wisdom.

Several years ago, I came across a Peanuts cartoon that I liked so much that I framed it and hung it on my wall. Lucy is sitting in her psychiatrist booth offering advice for five cents. Charlie Brown sits down and says, "See that plane up there? It's filled with people who are all going someplace . . . that's what I'd like to do . . . Go off someplace and start a new life." Lucy says, "Forget it, Charlie Brown you'd still be the same person you are." Charlie Brown says, "But maybe when I got to this new place, the new people would like me better." Lucy says, "Only until they got to know you Charlie Brown, then you'd be right back where you started."

Like Charlie Brown, many of us feel that when we transition, people will like us better. I believe that the same people who didn't like us in our old body will not like us in our new one. After all, it wasn't how we looked that made them dislike us; it was who we were and how we acted!

While I was not uncomfortable as a male, and I was generally well-liked by the people I knew, I found that after I transitioned, I was more sensitive to other people. I didn't expect people to be accommodating to me as I began my new life. Rather, I felt it was my obligation to be accommodating to them. Not that I was apologetic, but I felt that it was up to me to attempt to understand their confusion and lack of understanding. I tried to put them at ease, and not make them walk on eggshells in my presence.

Over the years I have known several people who were transitioning who were always angry about some perceived slight or insult. They were always upset when they were not accepted as women. Unfortunately, when you are tall, have broad shoulders, "man hands," and a deep voice, putting on a dress and wearing make-up will not cause people to regard you as female. Should this really matter? I didn't transition for them—I did it for me! It should be enough for ME to be happy with my new self. Everything and everyone else is a bonus!

I regard the world as my "mirror"! I look at others to see myself. If I don't like what I see, then it might be time for me to make some changes in myself. I have found during the last ten years since my SRS, people are always nice to me, just as I am always nice to them!

The moral of this story: No matter where you go, there you are!

Reasons

BRENDA

(FROM THE TS ROADMAP)

I'm a pre-op TS, not even full-time yet, mostly waiting on electrolysis. I'm going full-time by the end of the year, sooner depending on how job situations settle out.

I really like your site and would like to contribute some advice. I'm not sure where you would put it, because your focus is advice on people who have already transitioned in their teens or twenties (I just turned 28; I started when I was about 26). But I experimented and learned from a lot of mistakes when I was younger and looking into this process, and would like to relay some of what I learned in the process.

I'm not at the after-my-struggles-life-is-now-OK stage, but that doesn't mean I haven't learned from my own mistakes and the mistakes of others I've known who transitioned in their twenties. I would target my advice to people in their late teens or early twenties.

Take the time to be sure of what you want. While many of the physical effects of transition are reversible, over time they become less so, and certainly surgery is really not reversible. Keep in mind that if you transition, you are not just transitioning now at whatever age you are, but that you will be your target sex ten years, twenty years, many decades down the road.

Also keep in mind that, depending on whom you tell and at what points, you may not want to be "the kid who almost got a sex change."

Not that there's anything wrong with that. But I haven't met anyone who would really want to be that person.

A lot of people are lonely or estranged or disaffected in high school. If you feel this way already, transitioning is not going to help. Transitioning is not a good way to become cool or make lots of new friends (well, in some circles it might, but even then that's not the best reason). Don't make this decision out of desperation.

Be selective in your support. While there's more awareness of TS/TG issues, many people, even supportive people, will use you for their own purposes. Some people thinking it's cool to be friends with something "exotic" like a transsexual, or they want to prove how open-minded they are. Others—especially in feminist and queer theory circles—will use trannies as some sort of proof of one enlightened principle or another. Don't fall for it. Be yourself whatever you are.

Along similar lines, just because you are trans doesn't mean you should lower your standards to make friends. Remember that as you transition, whether openly or quietly, the people you hang out with are going to influence how you see the world, and how you see yourself. Find role models and peers who share values similar to your own. They can be trans or genetic girls; they can even be men.

"On this earth there is one thing which is dreadful. It is that everyone has his reasons." (Jean Renoir)

Many people transition, whether completely or partially, for a variety of reasons. Their reasons are not always yours; even two transsexuals who are the same age and background may have different reasons for wanting to change their sex. This is why therapy can be so important. You have to know your reasons for doing what you do. It's a good idea for everything, not just transition.

There are a lot of weirdoes out there. It's obvious that you don't want to be associated with them, but more important (and this would be my mistake) you don't want to let the weirdoes scare you away from the right decision. Conversely, you don't want to be overly supported into the wrong decision. The most important thing about transitioning is that YOU HAVE TO TAKE RESPONSIBILITY FOR YOUR OWN LIFE AND YOUR DECISIONS. Don't let anyone talk you into or out of what you are doing, and don't rush. If it's the right thing for you to do, you will be able to make your life situation fall into place and deal with your obstacles as they arise.

Know yourself and respect yourself and don't let anyone tell you what you are doing is wrong, selfish, dumb, goofy-looking, or whatever. If they say you're goofy-looking, check the mirror and decide what you like. That's just plain fashion sense.

Oh, one more thing: don't trust anyone over thirty.

My Silence, My Life

CHELLE MUNROE

Silence—sometimes a blessing, sometimes a detriment. I often wonder if I've yet to define which it is to me. It is a negative friend to which I have bonded by my own choice. No one actually forced me to be silent, I chose to be. I can't even begin to express the years that I remained silent while the real me was screaming to be born; to be free; to be happy; only to be denied because of fear of rejection by family; friends and co-workers. There were times when I let that fear fester to the point where I began questioning whether or not I was some kind of freak of nature. The numerous nights I spent alone crying until there were no more tears to shed. Even now, I hesitate to be my true self at times and suffer the guilt for not having the courage to open up and blossom. I hesitate to let go and be the woman I truly am in every cell of my body; in every beat of my heart; in every waking thought; in every moment.

Questions pop into my mind. How much longer are you going to let everyone else dictate your happiness? How many more years are you going to hide behind the veil of cowardice and live in loneliness and misery? How many more hours are you going to waste pondering the "what if's" of yesteryear? Yet, in spite of the questions and knowledge that my inaction will only cause sorrow, I still embrace that silence.

Now comes the reality that at age 63, I don't know how many years I have left. If I don't begin to live my life, truly live my life as it should be, I will die physically as I have died a thousand times over in my heart. Adrift in an ocean of a society that is discriminatory by nature, cold and hurtful because of ignorance and hate, and blinded by the need to force their views and beliefs on others—I desperately search for a lifeline to pull me to safety.

What scares me the most is my inability to ascertain whether I can break my lifelong habits of silence when that lifeline comes along. Right now, the transgender group I have joined is that lifeline and I find myself thrashing, clawing and reaching with every essence of my being to grasp hold of it while still clinging to the safety of my friend silence. We are reluctant friends for sure, but nevertheless, friends.

I will frequent this page, undoubtedly cry again and again, but for sure, I will find the strength in it to overcome the silence, one step at a time. I need to, or I'll forever be bound to a broken heart.

Now, more so than ever before, I realize through reading and listening to the news that the pain I have endured and still endure has been shared by so many before me. It is helping me to cope, and it is my sincerest hope that in some small way I too will serve to help those who are younger and struggling with the same silence and fears, that they may take the steps to reach out and touch base with those who really care. It may just make the difference between having a sad life or a happy one. Life is too precious to squander away as I have so learned—the hard way.

I wrote the letter above two years ago and have visited it often. I can now excitedly express that the silence has been broken as I live full time now as the female I have always known myself to be. Although I am still pre-op, I am experiencing more joy than I have ever felt in my life. The doors to the psychological prison that held me captive have been sprung open, and I am free—free to enjoy life to its fullest.

That is not to say that everything is fantastic. My brothers have not rejected me outright, but they have pretty much shunned me from the family, evidenced by my not getting an invitation to the annual family reunion cookout in August. Unlike other years, they also did not acknowledge my birthday this year. Naturally, these situations hurt, but I am on the road to the life that should have always been, and I am not making any U-turns or taking any exits that will lead me back to the silence.

One of the biggest and most joyous surprises I am experiencing in my journey is how so many people, who I never expected to, have welcomed and embraced me into their hearts. These precious gifts affirm my life and reinforce my resolve never to let go or to let it be taken from me again.

Hiding

JULIE WONG

I have done many stupid things in my life. Most of them didn't seem like stupid choices when I made them. There is one very stupid thing I made even more stupid by repeating it.

I would say that I always knew what I was. My earliest memories involve recognizing this difference or dealing with my difference in some way. I believed that everyone else could tell there was something wrong with me and that some might even know my secret. I guess that is the way of secrets. They keep consuming space in your life until there is no room for anything else.

Although I only used the word "transsexual" much later, I knew that I was one. This was my secret, and I kept it and hid it for as long as I could. I kept it until it darkened everything else in my life. When I finally let go of my secret, I discovered that what I believed was for my protection was ultimately hurting me. Hiding my secret was really hiding me.

I had created a person to inhabit. He was what I believed that others wanted me to be. He could be many things that I was not. He could be accepted and was worthy of love. My early experiences taught me I wasn't acceptable or worthy of love. For all the things he was, he still had many parts to his personality that were really mine. As I have come to learn, this is the nature of hiding. You can't stay hidden forever.

When I finally came out of hiding, it was glorious and frightening at the same time. Being present in my own life was the most liberating experience anyone could imagine. Everything in my world was new and different, and I had much of life to catch up on. It was also frightening because of many of the same reasons. I was new to this world and had no facade to protect me.

Those days of exploration were some of the best times I experienced, but I was eager to keep moving. I will say this to those at that early stage: stop and smell the roses. I wish that I had more time there. Moving on wasn't all that imperative. Those experiences are a confirmation of who you are that you will need to carry you through the rough times. Maybe the reason for my repeating this mistake was that I didn't experience all there was in that period.

Later, after I had completed my transition, I tired of being a transsexual. The coming out and explaining, discussions and desire to see pictures of me "before." I thought that I could never have an authentic life if all anyone saw was the facade I used to be.

I moved away to a new city, job, and life, leaving behind the part of me that transitioned. I had the dream of everyone that goes through a gender transition, no one knew I had been anything else but what they perceived me to be.

In order to maintain this life, I had to make a few changes. The sports I participated in during school became other activities. The friends from those times changed gender, names, and personalities. Pictures of me before disappeared or became a brother I never had. I felt I had to hate some things I used to like—the books I read, the movies I saw, the music I listened to. All of this needed to transition so that I could say I never did.

This was me repeating that mistake. I began to hide again. I lived behind a façade of a life. As I had done before, I began to censor myself and became more guarded about what I told people. Worse, I had to remember the lies.

I was hiding from who and what I was. Slowly I began the process of coming out again, and it was harder the second time. I had to not only explain being a transsexual, but also explain why I had kept it from them. I didn't have to tell everyone, just those people who were my closest friends.

I hope that you can learn from my mistake. You can't hide from who you are. If you know that you should transition but don't, you are hiding. If you have transitioned and you don't tell the people in your life, you are still hiding. I don't want to suggest that there isn't some danger in coming out. You do need to be careful about whom you tell, but not telling the right people can be just as bad. It will always be better to be yourself than something you are not.

That is the big lesson I have to teach. Being you is the most precious thing you can give yourself, and you are the greatest gift you can give to the world.

Strength

"You gain strength, courage and confidence by every experience in which you really stop to look fear in the face. You are able to say to yourself, 'I have lived through this horror. I can take the next thing that comes along.' . . . You must do the thing you think you cannot do."

— *Eleanor Roosevelt*

"The most difficult thing is the decision to act, the rest is merely tenacity. The fears are paper tigers. You can do anything you decide to do. You can act to change and control your life; and the procedure, the process is its own reward."

— *Amelia Earhart*

The Road I Traveled

JILLIAN ATKINS

I arrived at Key West airport on February 19, 1980, with one suitcase and $340 in my pocket, without a place to stay and no plan. I remember standing on the tarmac, the look of a lost puppy written all over me. It was 11:30pm and I was 19 years old. All I knew for sure, this was the only road I saw before me, and I took it. In a flash I traded the comfort of my family home and the softness of my bed for this sobering and quite scary moment.

With a stranger's hand on my shoulder and the offer of a place to stay, I was whisked away to my new reality, the gay community. Six weeks later I was parading around town dressed as a woman. My new friends were supportive, something that had been unfamiliar up to that point. Still, I was very much alone in my struggle to reach womanhood. Looking back I realize I put myself in some compromising situations that could have gone terribly wrong. Naivety is my only excuse, and I was so desperate to be accepted and validated as female.

I was a quick study. The femininity that had been hiding was released and blossomed. Several months later I was on a bus to New York City. This was the place where money and sexual favors became my daily existence. Two years later I had enough for the final surgery. During that time the hormones flowed, and at one point I was taking three different kinds all in the pursuit of womanly features. All the twists and turns had made it well worth the final moment of my transition. I had a newly revised body, but the same old shame was still there, carried over from the 19 year old who had left home in search of herself. The sight of my reflection in the mirror, the attention I received from men, and the opportunities that came with being a beautiful young woman, placated the old wounds. I lived on the fringe, resenting the society that condemned me and those like me, while the whole time I used my beauty and ability to "pass" as a means of fitting into that society, hiding my past at all cost. In my private moments, I always had a fear of discovery and a wounded heart that longed for validation.

Somewhere I had let the shame and rejection I felt diminish that vision, and I wound up slithering through a disenfranchised existence to cross the finish line. But just when you think you are finished after recovering from the surgery that finalizes the journey, you discover that there is more work to do. It took years for me to realize that living in stealth was a double-edged sword that kept me tethered to my shame. Secrets and fears ruled my decisions, and kept that scared 19 year old a prisoner in my mind and heart.

Where was the education I had wanted? Where was the strong confident woman I had envisioned who would stand up and be counted? Where was fulfillment of my true potential? I often wonder if could have reached that destination in any other way given the times and places in which I found myself. We all get to womanhood in our own way and have to deal with a multitude of issues that has no real recipe.

Follow your heart and take the road deemed necessary for you and you alone. Don't lose who you are. Face the shame and fight it head-on. The road is long but has many gifts along its bumpy path if you open your heart to making the world a better place for you and others.

May the Universe watch over you, my sisters.

What I Did Right

ANONYMOUS
(FROM THE TS ROADMAP)

The four smartest things I did during transition were:

1. I worked on self-acceptance early on, first thing, before I saw my first therapist or took my first hormone tablet. This was the most important thing I ever did. I realized early on that all the surgery in the world could only do so much, and that the most important transition work would take place within me. I came to accept the things about me that couldn't be changed, no matter what. I could either be miserable about what I had, or I could make the most of it. Accepting myself, and becoming comfortable with myself, made the rest of the journey a whole lot easier.

2. I held on to myself and to the other things that made life interesting. Sure, transition's a big thing, and it has a huge effect on everything in your life. It certainly did in mine. But, even with all that, I needed time for my other passions in life. Sometimes there's a temptation to say, "Well, I'm changing genders, so that means I have to change interests and everything else." Some people do that because they genuinely want to, and that's perfectly fine. But it just wasn't me. I would have cashed in almost everything I cared about. I've been a tomboy all my life, anyway, and while

there are some "girl" things I love, there are some "girl" things I just can't get into. The real me wears blue jeans and old shirts most of the time, anyway. The key? Be yourself. Life's too short to force yourself into things you just can't dig. There's plenty of genetic women who love old cars and who fly airplanes, just as there's plenty of genetic men who like needlepoint and who take ballet lessons. All that is fine. We're all individuals, TS or not.

3. Over time I learned that there's no need to advertise myself as TS. I used to feel compelled to do it because I wanted to defuse the situation early on, get the issue out of the way and take out any awkwardness there might be. However, I later realized that sometimes introduced awkwardness—and, conversely, if I never brought it up, the issue probably wouldn't come up in most every-day interactions. There are instances when the issue does need to be brought up—medical care, intimate relationships, etc.—but common sense will tell you when it needs to be brought up, and with whom. Listen to that common sense.

4. How you project yourself is everything. I've not had one bit of surgery done on my face, but if I project "happy, confident young woman" then that's what people see and how they treat me. It's been enough to sustain me through job interviews, buying cars, traveling (under my old identity, no less), even sharing a room with several genetic females during a work-related trip. Nobody said anything about it—I was just one of the girls. I couldn't have done that had I acted nervous or been less than self-confident.

The three things I should have done better?

1. I wish I'd managed my money much better. I spent a lot of money in my transitioning years on things that now don't matter to me. I should have saved it up and applied it towards surgery and elec-trolysis. As a result, I had to reschedule my surgery three times over four years. It also would have made my post-transition life

easier, especially when it came time to buy real estate and the other necessities of life.

2. I wish I'd started electrolysis much sooner. It can be a very long process. It should have been the first thing I started on, but it wasn't. It's miserable being a woman with a decent face, a not-bad body, and a wonderful new state-of-the-art vagina . . . but who has to shave each morning. Ewww.

3. I wish I'd just generally been a lot smarter, especially early on, when it came to dating and relationships with men. It's easy to be so starved for acceptance that you let yourself be used by people who only want you as an exotic conquest. I had one incident early in my transition with a guy who, it turned out, just wanted to have sex with me, and it left some emotional scars for a while. Of everybody I was mad at, I was most upset at myself for letting it happen. There are some wonderful guys out there who will accept you, even after they know. They are worth waiting for. (The guy I'm married to is testament to that.) Don't, however, be so starved for acceptance that you settle for something that's bad for you. You have more dignity and self-worth than that. Be smart and be aware.

The T-word

DEVON

(FROM THE TS ROADMAP)

I am not a transsexual. I am transsexual. See the difference? Although it may seem subtle, there is a vast difference, with complex philosophical and social implications. Understanding this difference is essential to understanding ourselves and how we fit into society.

In the first instance, "transsexual" is used as a noun; in the second, as an adjective. One significant problem with use of the noun form is that it replaces gender completely. Instead of being referred to as men and women, or even transsexual men and women, we are called simply transsexuals—in effect, invalidating our gender. The following exchange between two male characters in a television program I watched recently illustrates this point:

"Who's that woman over there?"

"That's a transsexual."

Notice that his response was not "That's a transsexual woman," or "She's transsexual." The implication is that a transsexual is not a woman. Using "transsexual" as a noun divests people of their basic, essential qualities—man, woman, or even person. Thus, it dispossesses, and often, dehumanizes. In many cases, that's the objective, the implicit goal.

The power of language to shape perceptions, opinions, and behavior has long been recognized. Thought processes at a basic level are extremely susceptible to manipulation by language. Advertising and political propaganda depend largely on language's ability to influence, for questionable purposes. Likewise, perceptions about those who have changed sex are forged by language. To our detriment, the prevalent use of "transsexual" as a noun has not had a positive impact on these perceptions.

Nouns are the primary components of speech, and they possess greater power and more potential for abuse than any other element. Consider this example: "a black man" versus "a black." The second construction strips the individual of his status as a man, an insidious thing. However, when the same word is used as an adjective modifier the problem disappears; "black" then simply describes the noun "man," the most important component of the sentence. Similarly, when "transsexual" is used as an adjective the implicit meaning changes—the emphasis is placed on person, man, or woman first, transsexual second.

It's important to note that the adjective and noun forms of "transsexual" have different connotations. The adjective's meaning and implications are, by comparison, benign. The noun is easily co-opted as a slur; it lends itself all too readily for use as an epithet. The phrase "That's a transsexual" is easily infused with derogatory implication, and even when this is not the intent an undesirable connotation remains. The adjective form, "That's a transsexual person," has far less power to disparage than does "That's a transsexual," even if that is the speaker's objective. Try saying both phrases yourself, as contemptuously as possible, and compare the slur-quotient of each.

Adding considerably to the problem is the word "transsexual" itself, or more specifically, one of its components. Any noun that ends in "sexual" is unavoidably imbued with a great many negative connotations. "Transsexual" is tainted by this unfortunate characteristic, as are "homosexual" and "bisexual." Somehow this trait ensnares and contaminates us even more when the noun form is used. So that makes three strikes against it.

Popular abbreviations are also a cause for concern: "trannies," "transies," "T's"—all these terms should make us cringe, for the same reasons as the noun from which they are derived. While we're on the subject, we also should not be enamored with "trans-men," "trans-women," and "trans-people." These labels are subtly denigrating; let's expunge these rascals as well.

Intersexed people faced a similar problem with language when they were called "hermaphrodites." After years of being saddled with this repellent, sinister-sounding label, they finally decided they'd had enough. Letting it be known that the use of "hermaphrodite" was unacceptable, they insisted that "intersexed" should be used instead. (And another struggle may lie ahead for them if the use of "intersexual" as a noun becomes prevalent.) As a result, it has gradually come to be considered insensitive and politically incorrect to use the old term. We should applaud them for recognizing the disservice it caused them and then doing something about it. Furthermore, we need to take a lesson from them; they have shown us it is possible to change the language.

It's crucial that we wake up and realize that language can do us tremendous harm when misused. Sinister things can sometimes be very subtle, and cause great damage before they are perceived as detrimental. For our own well-being we must learn to be discriminating about the use of language as it applies to us. Whether to use a word as a noun or an adjective may seem to be a subtle distinction, and therein lay the danger. Make no mistake about it, the use of "transsexual" as a noun injures us, as individuals and as a group. It is often employed as a weapon by those who seek our destruction. Its use divests us of our identity and personhood, dispossesses us, and vilifies us.

If we show the resolve demonstrated by intersexed people, we can look forward to the day when calling someone a transsexual is seen as politically incorrect. On that day we will have made a significant gain. In the meantime, we must make sure the language we ourselves use does not make us accessories to our own debasement. We are transsexual—transsexual women, transsexual men, transsexual people. We are not transsexuals.

Dear 15 Year-Old Me

ZOE BRAIN

I can do nothing for you, the 15 year-old girl that I was, silently sobbing in your bedroom. Back in 1973, I know your parents wouldn't understand. I know from the current year (though you don't, and perhaps that's for the best) that if you let your secret out, the standard treatment in your time is electroshock therapy, sometimes even lobotomy, cutting out pieces of your brain, so best keep quiet.

I can do nothing for you, but I can do something for all the girls like you who exist in my time. Knowing me, knowing you, the girl I was I think that will make you smile amidst your tears. It's how I soothe the hurt that you're feeling, easing the path of others.

It will take a long time I'm afraid, but you'll live happily ever after, too, as they will. We have a better understanding now. We have something called the Internet. It links all the computers in the world, and every home has at least one now. We use it to share information. The surgery is far better, the knowledge of hormones more extensive. We can't give girls like you the ability to have babies, not yet, but that's coming too. Too late for you—for us—but perhaps not too late for those who follow us.

It's no easier for other girls at 15 than it is for you, back in 1973, stuck with a male body that feels so terribly, fundamentally WRONG. But there is hope for them, as there doesn't appear to be for you, in your time. After living for so many years, hoping even when there is no hope, you get to win anyway, to be yourself. You will learn what the word happiness means. It will be better than you can imagine, better than your wildest dreams. Against all the odds, you get to live happily ever after.

You have many years of hell in front of you. Far too many. But it's not forever.

Today, girls like you don't have to endure nearly so long. If they can endure, just for another thousand days, there will be help available for them. No child should have to endure what you are destined to endure, but you get through it. No child should have to endure even one thousand days of it, nor one thousand seconds for that matter. They do have to, though, at the moment. It's changing, getting better, and I think in my—in our—lifetime, we'll see an end to it. The issue will be recognized earlier, and social acceptance of the obvious treatment will become unremarkable. That day is not here yet, which is why we, you and I, have to help them.

You and I just have to show the girls of today who are your age that there is hope. That it does get better, and by the time they're 25, their lives will be not much different from other girls their age. That's not some impossible dream, not just a possibility, it's an inevitability, if they just hang on. Meanwhile, they must lay the foundations of their future lives, do well at school, be ready to make a fantastic success of life, and not fall into the traps of drug abuse or throwing away a life that at the moment seems worthless. We must show them that they must plan ahead, for the better times to come for them.

They may end up marrying boys, and having a family together. Or marrying girls for that matter—we've come a long way in understanding sexuality since 1973, and same-sex partnerships, while unusual, aren't regarded as unthinkable as they were.

Dear 15 year-old me, feeling so isolated and alone back in 1973, you don't know that there are many like you. Boys and girls, born with the wrong-sexed bodies. Yes, there are boys too, born with female anatomy, and it's just as horrid for them as it is for girls born with male anatomy. Now, we do know though, and we are doing something about it. There's still plenty of bullying (and worse than bullying) in schools, and not just from other kids. That's getting better though, too. The trouble is that's little consolation for all the 15 year-old boys and girls subjected to it today, so we have to show them that others have made it, and they can, too. That it gets better, and not in ten or twenty years, but in just a few. They should be busy preparing for that day.

I hope I've made you smile, dear 15 year-old me. You get to be quite a woman, you know? You use the pain you're feeling now as an energy to help others just like you, transmuting it into compassion. Writing letters like this one.

Love, and Hugs,
Zoe

Dear Penis

DIANNE CHAPMAN

Dear Penis,

You and I have been together for a long time. I cannot remember a time when you were not with me. After all our time together, I am afraid that our relationship must change.

In my early days, I never gave you much thought. Until my sister pointed you out as the difference between girls and boys, I had no reason to think about you at all. Now I couldn't help but notice you. I didn't know how to feel about you, and you made me feel inadequate and incomplete. I tried to hide you and started to pretend that you were not there.

It would be a few years before you intruded in my life again. Now it was harder to ignore you. It seemed that even though I kept you hidden, others could tell you were there. They were treating me differently because of you. It seemed that no matter what I really was, I couldn't convince them because of you. Now the only time I could be myself was when I was alone.

More years passed, and now your influence was growing. Because of you more of my body was changing in ways that made it harder for even me to see who I really was. I was powerless to stop the changes you were effecting on my life. Now I felt trapped in a body and life that was not mine. The helplessness turned to sadness and anger. The only remaining place for me to live was in my imagination.

Life wore on and you remained with me. In desperation for fresh air and the light of day, I searched for a way out of my prison. Finally I found a ray of hope; there were others like me. It took a while to find the pieces to the puzzle. I knew that others had made it, and that made it possible. Eventually, I came to believe that what was possible for others could be possible for me. It would not be easy but there was hope.

Amid the joy of freedom lurked a nagging fear, your fear. The life that was yours would need to end for my life to begin. You feared that would be the end of you. Like your physical manifestations, the feelings of fear you brought would poke through now and again, interrupting my thoughts, hopes and dreams. I found that I could hold off your fears by focusing on the life I should have had by birthright.

I am truly sorry for those things that I said about you to all the therapists. They were truly horrible and hurt you greatly. I wished that I didn't have to say them, but I couldn't get others to understand. They held sway on my future and yet could not grasp the true nature of our relationship. I held out as long as I could, but they insisted. It was the only way they would allow me to live.

The change in hormones has started to reverse the damage you have done. Although there are things that cannot be reversed, these changes are welcome. Best of all, they silence you. They allow me to be your master now. You can no longer pop up whenever you like. The only time you have is by my choice now, no longer will you intrude. I will keep moving into the life I see in front of me.

When I reached the final stage, your fears magnified. Your very existence was being threatened. I understood because I could remember how you had threatened mine. Yet I couldn't stop, I couldn't slow down. All the plans had been laid out at great expense. My journey was reaching the desired conclusion. I can accept your end, as it mean that I can be whole.

But after it all, you are still here. Not gone, not dead, simply transformed as I have been. You can be whole within me as I am whole within the world. Although our roles are reversed there was nothing to fear. I have a new purpose for you and I look forward to the things that we can do together. A new life awaits us both. A life with room enough for us both to live.

Life after You Are Done

EMILY
(FROM TS ROADMAP)

When I reflect on adjusting to life once the mechanical aspects of transition are over, the healing of surgery and such behind us, I am reminded of a passage from Dr. Martha Stout's *The Myth of Sanity: Divided Consciousness and the Promise of Awareness*. Dr. Stout discusses dissociative identity disorder (DID) but surprisingly, much of what she writes is relevant to growing up with, and finding a way to cope with, finding one's self being told they belong to one gender, yet identifying internally with the other (which is what I think of when I read GID: gender identity disorder), and the resultant intense dysphoria. Perhaps the relevance of DID to GID is not remarkable considering most men and women who grow up grappling with transsexualism exist internally as one person and externally as another, at least until transition. Even if this passage is not entirely germane, I find it thought provoking and worth including nonetheless. Paraphrasing and modifying slightly what she writes:

People [surviving transsexualism] have usually survived the unsurvivable whether recognized or not. They did not fail to thrive and so perish in childhood, as one might reasonably have expected, nor did they commit suicide in adolescence, another bitterly common result. No, they divided themselves, and they survived; and the fact that they survived, and in many cases survived well, probably means that as a group they tend to be, by their original nature, people who have exceptional gifts. Typically they possess intellectual, interpersonal, or creative abilities that might have set them apart from the crowd even if (especially if) their histories had been different. They are superadapters, mind boggling really.

But there is inestimable waste, the waste of a very bright candle at which tragic circumstance has for too long blown a heavy, near extinguishing mist. The flame may hiss and flash large at times, in impossible displays of protest and vitality that are compelling to witness, but it is always in danger of fading to black.

The talents I refer to are inborn; trauma does not bestow them. Trauma is merely the cruel taskmaster. It rivets our attention but is no giver of gifts.

More generally there is the issue whether or not psychological pain bestows or perhaps enhances creativity, an old debate. It is the question of, for example, "Would a happy Charles Dickens have written *A Tale of Two Cities*?" In working for many years with a great many traumatized people, artists, musicians and writers among them, I have answered this question to my own satisfaction, and my answer is this: I do not think a happy Charles Dickens would have done less brilliant work, particularly if he were happy because he has recovered from being unhappy. On the contrary, I think the natural genius of Charles Dickens would have expressed itself even more luminously and also that the people around him would have led far more comfortable lives.

Happiness is not a mixed blessing.

I tell this opinion to those of my patients who fear they will lose a certain creative edge should they be "cured." One does not lose one's edge. If anything, it becomes a finer blade, and (the best part) one does not have to bleed for it nearly so much. A talented person is not talented because of her or his pain. She or he is talented despite it. The pain is like a gauzy gray mist that has wrapped itself several times around a priceless clear light."

As for me, the first great challenge in adjusting to life once the obvious and formidable physical goals were reached was to learn how to trust myself and my authenticity as a woman. This involved mastering fears, most of which spring from not having been validated as a woman growing up. I may have enviously observed other women from childhood on, and even vicariously experienced certain aspects of womanhood through my friendship with other women, but I had no personal cultural frame of reference through which to define and measure what it means for me to be a woman. Until I could do this, I was plagued with fears I would not assimilate and enjoy a normal life as just another woman.

I found online and through local support groups helpful information while planning, then carrying out my transition. Ultimately, however, these were for me way stations on the longer journey towards self-acceptance and actualization as a woman. When young girls approach puberty, they start to engage in assuming the role of a young woman. They experiment with dress, make-up and personality in an effort to try on various "ways of being" that change and evolve throughout young adulthood until a sense of their selves as women crystallizes. For me this experience was carried out online and through support groups, and of course graduating and then venturing out into the world on my own, making mistakes and learning from them. At some point you glean all you can, if anything, from those online and support groups and for better or worse strike out on your own. You cannot define yourself as a woman in society through online and real world support groups, though some make a home of what for most is a way station to happier vistas.

My greatest joy and most useful healing occurred after I stopped spending time in these way stations and began forming relationships with men and woman in the world around me. In making friendships, some deep, most superficial, with other women in particular, I find great peace. I've come to understand that my former sense of what it meant to be a woman was narrow, almost a caricature, though the mistake was innocent and easy to make looking from the outside in, as I did so much of my life growing up. In the locker room I have seen body shapes so many and varied that I finally shed the self-consciousness of my own body, and with it, a heavy yoke of fear I'd been carrying. In the spectrum of women I've met as friends and acquaintances, I've come to understand how (in this day and age at least) so much of my past, which I feared might be seen as contrary to being a woman, is not incongruous. As a result I can speak freely of skills and interests which make up an important part of who I am, which is to say I need omit little of my life, or fabricate some false history, cloaking for example my love and interest of mathematics, or my familiarity and comfort with matters mechanical. I understand now, reflecting on my past and life growing up, that like all women, I fought battles to define myself; the only difference is mine was on unconventional fronts. Peer to peer relationships with other women provide me with a healthier, confident lens through which to see the entirety of my life.

What I am trying not very successfully to say is that my relationship with other women as a woman helped me to find my place in the tribe of women, to feel comfortable about who I am and where I fit in the fabric of society. I could not find this same solace and certainty in online discussion or real world support groups. Initially, while I found acceptance in these places, eventually I came to feel as if they were the blind leading the blind, or worse, self-appointed "experts" of womanhood who rarely left their dark caves to venture into the wider world of women. They harshly judged and filled with doubts those of us who wanted only to heal and assimilate.

My relationships with men are rewarding now, as well. Though in the context of overcoming fear they were most useful in giving me the validation I desired as a woman. I craved this validation like a person craving water emerging from the desert. It is scary and difficult to find yourself starting your thirties and going on your first date. But those leaps into the unknown, and the numerous mistakes I made that now make me blush with nostalgic embarrassment, were vital in quenching the white hot anxiety that pierced my heart and flamed my doubts in myself. I dated both men and women because I had no clear sense of what I wanted and I needed to try all avenues once my body was in line with my spirit. While my experiences with certain men are more recent than many of my female friends, we all share memories with men while we were finding ourselves as women that make our eyes roll now, or that we laugh about over drinks. Also, like many women I know, the journey to find myself sexually and as a woman is ongoing. This path of sexual self-discovery is another thing I find comforting to see in others my own age.

Shifting gears, I want to speak for a moment about another aspect of my adjustment to life after surgery, something that other women don't experience. I gave myself permission with my closest friends, those who knew how difficult my journey to self was, to share and speak of the joy and wonder I felt once the gauzy gray mist wrapped around my own piercing light as a woman had been removed. Opening myself up to this private happiness was important, and I am fortunate to have a few in my life with whom I could share my innocent delight. Happiness is always healing, and I urge all to find it wherever they may, regardless of the form, or what others may think. This is your own journey—listen if you like and digest what others have to say, but do with it what you will and never be afraid to be an iconoclast.

Tears

GINA WHITE

I pretty much never cried in the past. It took something completely traumatic, like the death of a friend, to make me cry.

So I was completely caught by surprise when I found myself sobbing uncontrollably in a conversation with my domme. Sobbing uncontrollably three different times in that one conversation. She was lovely about it, gracefully making me feel cared for.

This marked a change in me. Since then I have been venturing into even more femininity, being out with more people. It has been wonderful overall. It has also brought more tears. Sometimes because I am sad, sometimes because I am scared, and sometimes because I am so very happy.

I now find that I cry easily. I also find that it is such a release to cry. To be comforted by someone who cares about you, while you cry, is to be given a great gift. I've learned that tears of joy are a real thing.

At first I thought of this as something I should expect to get past. I thought that I should be patient with myself, and that given some time, I would become more balanced and then I would go back to not crying, and I thought that would be a good thing.

Now I look at it as something I don't want to give up at all. I want to feel all of these emotions. I want to be comforted, and I want to comfort others. Something has broken free inside of me, and I am better because of it.

I've learned that some people are much, much better at comforting me when I cry than others. I've realized that I tend to freeze up when other people cry. I want to learn to be more at peace with someone else crying, letting them feel the emotions and making them feel comforted and cared for.

You're Not Crazy

KELLY O.

What I am about to tell you will not be popular with many people. The same people will not understand what I have to say at all. It's all right that they don't like or understand it, this is not for them. It is for you.

You are not crazy!

There are people with college degrees who will authoritatively tell you to your face and in print that you are sick, you need to be examined, tested and verified. They are wrong. You are not crazy.

You will have to submit to the indignity of their process to gain access to the services you need. You will pay their fees and listen to them tell you how to do what they haven't done themselves. They pretend to be your friend, but you don't need a friend on a billable hour basis. They will insist that you need to stay, that you need their help, but you just need them to get out of the way. You need to be you, and you are not crazy.

Others will say that they can "fix" you and make you like being who you are not. They think that your gender is delusion, and if caught early enough, can be cured. They want to make you go away. They want you dead. In time everyone will see they are the ones with the delusion, they are the ones who are disordered, and you are not crazy.

Someday we will be free. When we no longer need them, when we no longer pay them, they will be gone. Their care and concern will fade, and we will see that they were not our friends, they were our oppressors. They will never repay the thirty pieces of silver they got for their work. They will never apologize for the wrongs they inflicted or the damage they have done.

It will simply be over, and you still will not be crazy!

"If a plant cannot live according to its nature, it dies; and so a man," wrote Henry David Thoreau.

P.S. Sigmund Freud, I think the existence of transwomen disproves the whole "penis envy" thing. We had them, and we are better without them! Truth is women don't really want to own penises; they are too much work. We would just like to rent one every now and then!

P.S. Carl Jung, You are just too into yourself, it's not healthy, dude! Stop the hallucinogens, and focus on reality. You don't have to be crazy to work with them!

Hope

"We dream to give ourselves hope. To stop dreaming—well, that's like saying you can never change your fate."

— *Amy Tan*

"Hope is the thing with feathers-
That perches in the soul-
And sings the tune without the words-
And never stops at all"

— *Emily Dickinson*

Dear Calpernia

Dear Calpernia,

It's the early 1980s, there is no internet to speak of in Nashville, Tennessee, and pretty much everybody in the South is going to hate you if you tell them that you're starting to feel like you need to be a girl. You're kinda screwed, and I get that. I'm not going to sugar coat this, so listen up. As you already know, it's life and death. And we don't have a lot of time.

I'm not going to lie to you. This is no grade school health class handout. I will, however, leave out a lot of things that are too real to put into writing. I can't help you with everything, and that's a lesson to be learned in itself.

First, don't kill yourself. I know you think about it every single day. I know there are reams of pages in your diary (the blue one wrapped in Chinese silk with your girl name written inside) that are covered in those two words, written again and again in different secret languages that only you and your brother can read: "Kill yourself." But don't.

Believe it or not, yes: Ugly, skinny, tall, buck-toothed, fish-mouthed, acne-spotted, socially-hopeless, dirt-poor, ignorant YOU will become a reasonably nice looking blonde girl with bountiful curves and enough charm to make a living from strangers who will pay to spend an hour

65

or two watching you perform every weekend for the next two decades, at least.

If you could see me, your future self, sitting here writing this letter, you probably wouldn't believe it. By the time you're here, you will have traveled the world, performed for crowds of thousands and you will have been called "beautiful" both by strangers and by people who love you very much. (I know that's important to you). Glittering crowns will be placed upon your head, countless stacks of (small-bill) money will pass through your hands and celebrities who you are currently not even allowed to watch on television will someday invite you to their homes and call you a friend. There are so many good things waiting to happen to you. I still can't believe them now, but trust me it will be exciting. You'll fuck a lot of it up, and squander a lot of it, but that's a part of it, too. Enjoy it all.

Mom and Dad currently have you bound up in the ludicrous trap of religion, so tightly that you will be crippled by it a little bit for the rest of your life, but guess what? They will get old. They will get sick. They will get weak. They will even forget just exactly what it was that they did that was so terrible, so that really the only person in the world who holds onto it is you. In many ways, that will be even more infuriating.

But someday, they will need you. Your new life will be incomprehensible to them, but as old age creeps in and health slips away, even your radically altered form will coalesce into the vision all straight heterosexual parents seem to have for their kids: You were their selfish bid for immortality, and their fading, increasingly vaporous hands will reach out to you with ever more urgency as they feel their lives slipping away, to prove to themselves that some part of them will still be here on Earth even when they expire like a snuffed match and the burnt stick is thrown away. The verdict is still out on how you'll handle that, but just know that they are paper tigers that you can tear up or press into your scrapbook as you wish, when the day comes.

In the future, some will take a page from Nancy Reagan's "Just Say No!" campaign and tell kids like you that "It Gets Better." But I won't lie to you. It just won't. Nothing really "gets better." Here's what happens: It doesn't get better. You just get stronger. I know you feel so weak and lonely right now, but you will discover over the years that you simply lack the ability to stop. Sometimes you will desperately want to stop, and in those moments, it will feel like a terrible curse. But at other times, you will find yourself still going after indescribably heart-breaking tragedies and be glad that you still have time to try and see if something better is coming.

I have to go, stuff is still happening, and it just never seems to slow down. A few last thoughts: PLEASE focus on your education because you'll need it when everyone abandons you during the early years. Start transitioning as early as possible; you can get hormones though mail order. Do not EVER consider getting silicone injections in your face. Be picky about who you have sex with. Keep your head down and your powder dry. Be ready to fight, literally and figuratively. People can be monsters. Find the good ones, and never let go.

> With stern, hopeful love,
> Calpernia

For Marlene, love Jenn

JENN DOLARI

Hi Marlene,

I t should be the evening of January 9th, 1995, when you get this. I want to say I hope this letter will find you in good spirits, but I know better. If I remember right, you've just talked with your closest friend, and you have a lot to think about. She's said some good things, and you should talk with her more when you get the chance.

Now, I know it's been a rough day, and you could use a few moments to relax. That's why you're out here under the stars in the middle of nowhere. A bit of peace. To be honest, I do this too. I was just out in the middle of the Texas Hill Country, parked up on a hill watching a thunderstorm fifty miles away moving across the horizon with the Milky Way flowing behind it. The dark, the quiet rumbles. It drains the stress away.

But that's just me. We should talk about you. Let's sit for a bit and talk about a few things while we enjoy the dark and quiet.

I know this day hasn't gone well. You got your college grades today, and, well, no one is going to be happy with those. On top of that, you quit your job after nearly throwing a punch at your boss. Totally not blaming you for that. Really, he would have deserved that, no doubt. He hasn't really helped your morale. The punch might have, but at least you're out here under the stars and not in jail for assault.

That's never a great way to end an evening. But I know you. There's more. Much more.

You're transgendered. Yes, I know you're trans. Trust me, it's not the secret you think it is. It's okay, though. The right people know. And those right people know what it's done to you, and how you've suffered, and how the path you're going down got so dark. The pain, and even hate, that put you out here under the stars to find a little peace.

There now. Had a little banter back and forth, yes? We're good friends now, right? Awesome. Cause I'm going to let you in on a little secret. This letter is coming to you from the year 2013. The miraculous world of tomorrow, where computers have more than 256 colors, cell phones are the size of a deck of cards, and your Game Boy is in 3D. Seriously. 3D Super Mario. Who'da thunk it?

Nonononono! Wait, wait, wait! Don't put down the letter. Hear me out. You watched Dr. Who. You know how that whole wibbly wobbly timey wimey thing works. Just . . . just hear me out. Just for a few seconds more. In fact, just for three more words.

You make it.

Still there? Good.

That's right. You make it. You don't get everything you want. You don't get everything you need. And it takes a while, yes. But you do get a bit of peace in the end.

It won't be the easiest trip you're going to take to get there. It never is. But nothing good is ever just handed to you on a silver platter, unless the restaurant has four stars. It's going to take a lot of hard work, and a more than a bit of suffering that may make today seem like a cakewalk.

You're going to leave your home, not once but twice. You're going to be discriminated against. You'll be insulted to your face, have your food messed with. You will come face to face with the law.

But you'll also have great adventures ahead of you. You're going to have the best ice cream in the world at the Penn State Creamery. You're going to drive halfway up Mount Rainier, in the very same blue pickup that brought you out here. The one you'll one day name Cheyenne. You're going to fall deeply in love, not just with the most beautiful soul in the world, but with a job you can't even imagine you'll be getting. You're going to find a family you didn't know you had, and understand another family you'd completely misjudged. And best of all, you'll come home. Not once, but twice.

Along the way, you'll create things. They won't be the TV series you'd always envisioned, or the plethora of comic books you'd planned to draw out. In fact, they won't be very big things at all. But even small things help. They help not just you, but also others in your very same situation. It's not anything special. At least you won't feel that way. But many people you know, and even more you don't know, will find solace in what you do.

But most of all, you're going to make it. Eventually, you will have your hormones, you will have your name changed (Marlene's a little old fashioned, don't you think?). You're going to grow breasts and slam them into doorframes. You're going to wear skirts and blouses with confidence. You're really gonna like wearing fashionable boots. You won't be accepted by every woman out there. But you'll be accepted by most women. It happens. I've seen it. And it's enough.

I've seen the years between here and there. It'll be rough, but you're going to do great Marlene. You just have to keep moving forward for it to happen. If you can just keep taking one step at a time, you'll make it to the miraculous world of tomorrow, where computers have more than 256 colors, cell phones are the size of a deck of cards, and your Game Boy is in 3D. It's like you can just reach in and grab Chun-Li! Seriously!

Anyways . . . I do have one small request, if you don't mind. Please take the gun out of your mouth. If you don't, you won't be able to give yourself the time to have the adventures (and the failures) that will make your life worth living down the road. Putting the gun down now will start you down the path to making your life into the one I have now. And I promise you, in the end, you won't regret it.

If you'll just put that gun down, I'll see you in eighteen years. Trust me.

Jenn

This Day

CARRIE GARCIA

This day isn't like any other day. Not today literally, but today five years ago. It's the day that I wanted to quit everything. It's funny that a single day a lifetime ago can be something that I will always remember.

It started innocent enough, talking with Teresa. We met during our freshman year. I admired her; she was such a free spirit and a lesbian. Not an easy thing with a Hispanic family. At first she thought that I was hitting on her. When she finally got to know me, she thought that I was gay. Sometimes we pick our role models, and sometimes they pick us.

I said that we were talking. It was more like arguing. She was insistent that I come out to my parents. She had been out with everyone for a while now and thought it wasn't going to be a big deal for me. But being trans isn't like being gay. It's more complicated, less understood. We ended with words that we both regretted the moment they were spoken, and we parted.

Back at home, sitting in my room alone. Looking at the puzzle I had made from things I thought were important enough to keep in plain sight. There was the ambiguous stuff like my guitar. The butch stuff like my Xbox and the girl stuff like the bear that Teresa gave me from the carnival. Each item has a memory, emotion and purpose.

My earlier anger with Teresa is still strong, and the fear that I have about revealing myself to a world that is cruel and judgmental is just as heavy. All of these things are swimming with me in my room. I know she is right and I have to tell them. I just don't know how. I think of how much I am like the things in my room, a little of this, a little the other. The puzzle of the things reflects the puzzle of me.

I begin to see my problem. Like the things in my room, I have many memories, emotions, and purposes. All of them are going in different directions and tearing me apart with them. I need to be one.

Lost in myself there, the sound of my mother opening the front door breaks through. I quickly wipe the tears from my face and pick up the bear. Looking at it, I notice for the first time that it has an odd grin. Almost a smirk, but it has gentle eyes.

The scariest moment of my life. I go to my mother and say, "We have to talk."

I didn't quit. I didn't die. I am glad that I spoke up. I am glad that I told the right people. That was the moment that I began to live, really live. I still have the bear. Best of all, I still have my best friend, T.

Baggage Claim

ANGELA PALERMO

Dearest sisters,

I have a confession to make. Well, it may not be a confession so much as the giddiness of a sometimes timid adventurer: I love airports. I really do! So much activity, so many comings and goings. It's all very stimulating to my sometimes fevered imagination. (I am just old enough to remember a time when people went to airports just to watch the jets take off.) For me, travelers jetting off to fun and exciting locales like New York or Paris (or Cleveland!) more than makes up for the anxieties over security checkpoints and lost luggage. And whether I'm flying off myself or just picking people up at the terminal, I can't help but experience an adrenaline rush, even if only vicariously.

Very recently, I found myself "under the big top" at Denver International Airport, awaiting the arrival of someone I had not seen in person for over twelve years. She is a very special and important person in my life, no matter how upsetting her words and actions were over that intervening period. I love her and would do almost anything for her, despite her many flaws and foibles. I can't but do otherwise. She is no ordinary person. She is, well, my mother. The woman who birthed me into this world had been horribly abusive when I came out to her as a trans woman in July 2000 and refused to see me in person once her father was laid to rest in January 2001. Since my grandfather's passing, our relationship had been restricted to phone conversations on the six "nodal points" of the year: Thanksgiving, Christmas, Easter, her birthday, my birthday and Mother's Day.

No matter how well I adjusted to the "arm's length" treatment, no matter how much I told myself that this was "her issue, not mine," still this absence of direct, personal contact gnawed at me. It was the pro-verbial "thorn in my side." I went about my daily life, flourishing in my transition, but yet felt a yearning for a more positive and accepting atti-tude from my mother. I could not deny the hope that our relationship would grow closer, that she would finally "get over her shit." That hope remained strong, however much I placed it on the back burner out of emotional self-preservation.

So, there I was at DIA, waiting on a Friday morning in late October. I carefully noted on the way through the main terminal that my mom's flight would disgorge its baggage at Carousel 10. I hurried over to the appointed spot longing for a chance to see my mother's face in person, and to have her see mine, truly see mine, a woman's face looking back at her. Of course, I wanted her to respect my womanhood. And I just plain wanted to look good. Who doesn't, after all? For that reason, I'd had my hair styled the day before her arrival. I feel much more confident and "womanly" with a freshly done 'do. But I didn't want to look "too girly," so I wore jeans, a turtleneck sweater, and motorcycle boots. I thought femme with a touch of the "tough chick" would strike the appropriate balance. No need to shock my mother's sensibilities or stoke her anxieties over my trans status.

After waiting thirty minutes behind a metal railing, my mother's aged body ascended the escalator from the subterranean people mover station. She gave me a big smile and a wave, to my delight, and I did the same in return. All of a sudden, she began pointing, with great enthusi-asm, to her left. I was confused and puzzled by this, wondering what she was indicating. I thought she might have been telling me that she had to pick up her bags that way, but I knew that Carousel 10 lay in the opposite direction. I was so focused on her pointed finger that it took me a few seconds to recognize that my brother Joe was walking just to her left. I was, needless to say, stunned. My brother's reaction to my coming out as a trans woman had, in its own way, been as negative as my mother's. He had heaped his share of transphobic abuse on me. Our relationship had been frosty and not exactly filled with loving communication. It had been another casualty of my transition. But there he was, giving me a smile of his own. He had decided to come along about a month before the trip. They had kept that from me, thinking it would be a "nice surprise." Mission accomplished!

We ended up having a wonderful time together. I had invited my mom out for a housewarming party, and after some initial hesitation during which she again verbalized some aggressive transphobia (on my birthday, no less!), she accepted my invitation. I called her out on her transphobic spewing during that initial conversation, but calmly and respectfully renewed my invitation a month later. She actually seemed eager to see my new house, the first I had ever bought, and meet my (very trans positive) housemate Scarlet and other friends. I thought a "bricks and mortar" sort of thing just might get her over the hump of her longstanding transphobia. I have never been so pleased to be right!

Just over two weeks have passed since my family flew back to Florida. I'm still feeling the glow of a successful visit, of turning the page on a long and unpleasant chapter in our lives. I'm just so glad I never gave up on them, never angrily tossed them from my life, despite feeling tempted more than once. I've done my best to leave behind my own (internalized) transphobic "baggage" and held out hope that they would eventually do the same. In my case, patience (and resilience) paid off. The long wait is over. And right now, I'm seriously considering booking a flight to Florida for the holidays!

My Story

BARBARA KELLY

I am writing to my sisters, letting them know "you only live once." Do not let others control your life. This is a difficult enough journey.

I had SRS/GRS 34 years ago, back in the dark ages of transsexualism/ gender identity disorder. I NEVER regretted having surgery, I NEVER thought I had any options, being "myself," matching my mind with my body, was the only answer for me.

Back in the 1970's, most doctors knew nothing about transsexuals. It was so very different then. The Internet did not exist, there were not many help groups, and TS/TG groups were practically non-existent. Scary, yes . . . but I had to do what I had to do.

I was a college student in Florida when the conflict inside of me became unbearable. I studied and researched gender identity in the University library, looking through thousands of books and periodicals as much as I could. Remember, this was in 1970. There was very little written back then on the subject, but I just knew there had to be something out there. Finally, I came across an article about the Erickson Educational Foundation. I was excited to find that article and wrote to them immediately in hope they could help me. I received a letter back and to my joy they referred me to a local Psychologist in the Miami area. This person was one of the main reasons I am alive on this planet today,

I really believe she saved my life. . . After a year of therapy or so I was diagnosed with GID (Gender Identity Disorder). My depression was so extreme that doctors told me that I would have to leave Florida to get help in either a Gender Identity Clinic in Boston or San Francisco. Since Boston was closer, they chose Boston. I was packed up, put on a plane, and rushed off, barely having time to say goodbye to all my friends in Miami. It was April 1972.

I did receive help and began hormone therapy in Boston. It was hard, I knew no one. I eventually made it back to New Jersey, my home state. I was pricked and prodded by doctors there and used as their guinea pig. Eventually I was put into a State Mental hospital, just for "being TS." Thank god they can no longer do that in my state. I can remember the patients getting shock treatments. I was so scared I would be next.

I will NEVER forget that place. I can still smell that horrid musky odor in the corridors. They put me in a damp, cold, dark cell with a little peephole in the door. They took all my clothes and left me naked. Can you imagine how I felt? Someone who hated their physical body so much, being viewed through that peep hole in the door as a young "boy" by the primarily gay hospital guards. Staring at me, smirking, making abhorrent comments. I still have nightmares! It was the first time I ever saw my father cry, when he came to visit me there one day. My Dad was a macho tough guy. It was incredible for me to see him show such emotion for his child for the first time in my life.

It of course was hard time. I lost many friends, but I did have something many people like me did NOT have. After a 360-degree turn, I had the support of a loving, caring family. A religious family, but as I told my parents back then, "Would you rather have four daughters or three daughters and one dead son?"

Thank goodness they chose "four daughters"!

The number one surgeon at that time for people like myself, in Trinidad, Colorado, in 1979 did change my life forever, for which I am eternally grateful.

Yes, I am a survivor. I have helped many people transitioning these past 30 or so years. Just remember, it's a long hard, painful journey. It's not for many, but you surely will know what path to take if it's in your heart and your soul.

Barbara Kelly
St. Petersburg, Florida

The Foggy Road Home

BRIGID FALLON

When it came time to "face up" to my gender dysphoria, I was nearly 50. I'd always known that I was both male and female. I have a picture of myself at 18 months with a baby doll and toy train. Soon after, though, I learned to hide my more feminine desires and interests.

In truth, it never fully worked. Time went by with intermittent cross-dressing, a failed marriage, etc., etc. I finally tired of the fiction as middle age hit. Out with a friend one night I ran into a Tarot reader who confirmed for me the sense that I was living half a life. I knew that there was so much more to me than I'd explored, than I could explore as the man I'd become.

So I went to therapy, I got hairline implants, I took hormones. My face was lasered and I started going out "en femme." As my hair grew out I ditched the wigs, and I felt for a while that I was on my way to a fuller, more genuine expression of self. Expressing myself as a woman felt incredibly freeing, and I regretted each return to life as a male.

Incrementally I came out to my friends, and they voiced support and acceptance. Soon, however, they appeared to forget about the whole thing. Without instantly going full-time, I continued to present as the same person, which meant that when I asked them to address me in a more gender-neutral manner, they "forgot," or disregarded the request altogether. They continued to include me in comments about "you men."

My closest friend stated that I was not "passable" as a woman, and whenever I mentioned the transition, she insisted that I had always seemed more male than female to her. The reality reflected back to me by those I loved was painful. I suddenly saw myself as grotesque, my body feminized by the hormones, my face altered but grossly masculine and rapidly aging. My hair was wild and grey. I felt like a freak, alone as an unmoored boat, drifting and lost. And then things got worse.

By now the stories about jobs and homes lost during the financial crisis are common. Suffice to say that I ended 2010 with my income cut in half. My dear companion of 15 years, a black Lab named Hank, had just died. I lived in five different homes over a two-year span, carting my horses and cat all around the Portland Metro periphery.

With no insurance or money for doctor visits, I got cut off of estrogen. Gas prices continued to rise, and my trips to town as Brigid became fewer. My confidence fell, and the need to remain closeted in my new rural homes ate at me. It was, for a while, just so lonely and painful.

As I had done over the years, I began again to sit in the silence of my meditation, breathing the bright air in, out, in, out. Over time I felt my spirit grow, even as the false assumptions and vanity, shame and anger gave way with each exhale. I felt the layers of my constructed personality dropping away, my feminine spirit growing brighter, stronger, and clearer.

The attitude, swagger, and ego I'd developed were just so many lies. I let myself feel compassion, joy and connection independent of my outer circumstances. Over time I saw my gender identity and expression, my clothes and voice and name and pronouns, as relatively insignificant. Making way for Spirit to express itself was, is always the task at hand; becoming that fuller being was the point. Indeed, I now know that what we call gender is as fluid and synthetic as any social construct. All sorts of people in all sorts of places look and act counter to their assigned genders, classes, social groups, etc. We are much more than our designations would allow.

So now I have a good home, new work, and a new understanding of what it takes to live a genuine, open-hearted life. As a denouement to this period, I got my heart broken badly last year, and since then my view has been from a very hard floor of being. But with everything that's been stripped away from me and with all the new growth, things are much clearer, simpler and, in the end, more vibrant. I see the world with new eyes, and I have made lovely new friends. Even as I identify as an older, less "marketable" trans woman, there has actually been some dating.

Brigid's confidence is renewed, and my transition is re-igniting, though this time as an outgrowth, an expression of my deeper change. Electro has begun, the hair more coiffed and tamed. Phyto-estrogens now maintain my gains alongside anti-androgens. Mostly, though, I feel more connected to my genuine self. I feel prepared to re-enter life as a heartfelt, connected and joyful person. She is strong and beautiful, and I like her lots.

When Sexual Abuse Is Part of the Picture

SALLY DELLOW

Dear Sisters,

I am writing on a topic that receives scant attention in transition resources—the sexual abuse experienced by many trans* as young children. The sexual abuse and rape of adult trans* is also a major issue within our community. Although I wish to be specific about my experience as a child, this is not intended to diminish in any way the experience of adult trans* survivors.

It has taken me many years to be able to separate my identity as a trans-woman and the oppression I suffered because of this from the effects of the sexual abuse I suffered as a child and its effects. Teasing apart the two to answer the question: "Am I trans* because I was abused?" "Is my inability to form intimate relationships because I am trans*?" For me the answer to both these questions is now an emphatic "No!"

My story is complex because I have no clear memories of my abuse (just the fragments I do have are terrifying), but I can recall knowing I was a girl throughout my childhood and teenage years. So I attached many of the symptoms and reactions I now know can be attributed to the abuse to my trans-identity. I was poorly equipped to manage close relationships. I was defensive, scared, shy, and unable to fully connect with the people around me. I thought it was because I was trans and everyone could somehow see this.

My first attempt to deal with the abuse issues was around the age of thirty, but it did not work, in part because I was not dealing with my identity issues at the same time. Now twenty years later, I have tackled my identity issues first (I have been full-time in my preferred gender role for nearly twelve months now).

The legacy of the childhood sexual abuse has been in two areas in my life: a numbing of emotions or a lack of feeling, and the development of a stunted and warped sexuality. Both of these areas have been highlighted as my transition progresses.

The crying jags so often reported by trans-women during transition as the estrogen kicks in have been absent from journey. Tears are difficult to come by. I am slowly beginning to recognize different emotions: anxiety, joy, sadness, frustration, anger, pleasure, fun. In fact it has been recognizing "'good'" emotions that has driven my emotional recovery—who knew that feeling joy could feel so good! I've journeyed, from years of being numb to, bringing my emotions into consciousness and then learning to name them one by one.

I've been working on my sexuality. I have struggled to appreciate my body. It did not match my gender. It was my body that was abused, not me (the psychic split of dissociation). A body I despised. Sexuality is very closely tied to emotions and taking pleasure in my body. But my sexuality has been twisted and deformed into a heinous set of memories by the predatory behavior of a pedophile. If I am to heal, I need to recover my sexuality and make it my own. How do I construct a healthy sexuality from scratch when I am both trans* and a childhood sexual abuse survivor? Touch, skin on skin contact, is toxic for me.

Taking stock of my sexuality has been a challenge. Recognizing the damage that has been done and how this colored my subsequent experiences for forty years initially left me feeling devastated. Slowly I have built a picture of what I want my sexuality to look like, feel like and be like. Knowing where I was with my addictions and legacy of traumatic experiences, as well as having an idea of where I wanted to be, able to express a creative, sensuous, passionate sexuality, enabled me to begin my journey towards a healthy sexuality.

I have found positive expressions of an appropriate sexuality in literature, film, and music, using the creativity of others to create a positive framework for myself. I have been surprised by how effective reading novels, watching films and listening to music has been; I am starting to smile afterwards and seek out similar books and experiences. A little bit of positive reinforcement has done wonders.

Allowing myself to experience touch as a positive sensual experience is slowly occurring. Hugs from friends have become a weekly event. I am now slowly starting to explore skin-on-skin contact. Asking friends to simply hold my hand for a short time, but not long enough for me to become anxious. This is also setting up positive experiences around consent, something that was absent in the child-adult abuse setting.

My capacity to feel the ecstasy of a shared passion is increasing as I develop and expand my emotional range. The emotions I associate with my pre-transition sexuality are negative. As I have worked to create my own sexuality—as opposed to simply accepting the one that was imposed on me—I am experiencing happiness, joy and contentment, creating a new set of positive emotional experiences around my sexuality.

My determination to build a healthy sexuality that I can express is fierce. I express it with creativity, sensuality and passion. I have a journey in front of me that is every bit as important and difficult as transition. I cannot be the woman I am or the woman I want to be without healing the effects of the sexual abuse I suffered as a child. If you are a survivor too, please do not neglect your healing journey. It does get better.

Kind regards
Sally

Hate

HEATHER ALLEN

I have a confession to make. It is something that has been a source of shame that I have carried with me for years. I have hidden this away, but it's time for me to confess my sins. I have hate.

I was raised in a Christian family. We were not fanatics and not blind followers. My family truly believed in the teachings of my church. It was not the only church in our city, and we were aware of others and accepting of their different beliefs. These others were Christians and would be with us in heaven, but we knew that we were the ones that had the right teachings. There were non-Christians as well. We could tolerate the Jewish people, as they were OK because they had the right God, but we were better.

There were others and we knew that they were going to hell. They were going to hell because they didn't have the right God. We didn't look down on them. We pitied them. We would try to convert them and "save" them. But the worst of these were the people who were going to hell because of who they were. They were gay.

I thought I was gay, too, but I never told anyone. I didn't want to lose my family and friends. Most of all, I didn't want to go to hell. I prayed for God to save me from my affliction, but he wouldn't, couldn't, didn't. I asked that he would change me, but God was silent. I came close to telling someone, but experience had taught me that God could forgive a murderer but not someone like me.

91

I said that I had hate. I hated myself for who I was. So when a few of the boys from my church started teasing another boy in our school because he was "gay," I didn't say anything. And when their teasing turned to bullying, I still didn't say anything. And when they started hitting him, I was still silent. I was afraid. Afraid that they would know my secret, that they would do the same to me.

And now I hated myself even more. Now I hated myself for what I didn't do.

As I grew, I still prayed that God would save me. And God remained silent. I thought that it might be because I was unworthy. So I tried harder. I thought that if I just worked harder I could become good enough and God would love me. But I didn't love myself.

I went to school and studied hard. I wanted to be the good Christian that everyone thought I was. I spoke of love, redemption, and forgiveness, but none of these could ever be mine, because I wasn't worthy. I told others that God could help them solve any problem, but God couldn't help me solve mine.

People looked up to me. I was important. I was blessed. They said that I spoke for God. But God never spoke to me. Was it because God never loved me? Was it because I was unworthy? Was it because of my secret? These things ate away at my soul until I couldn't hold them back anymore.

I left the ministry and tried to find a place that I could just be me. Everywhere I went my secret was with me. I wanted to tell them, but I feared that if my new friends knew the truth they would turn me away. They would hate me. Why shouldn't they? God hated me and I hated me.

I stopped trying to be a good Christian, but I didn't know how. That was all I had ever been. I found other work and other friends and never told them about my past in the church. I found that they hated people like me. They just had other names for me. I had left everything I had known and still couldn't tell my secret.

I found myself back in that horrible thing that happened back in school. My new friends were taunting someone else but for the same reason. This time they weren't violent but they were mean. The man that they hated wasn't a bad person. I had seen him around. He worked somewhere near us, and I remember him being kind to the homeless people on the street. In church we called that love.

I drew my courage into me. I stepped between my new friends and this man. I told them they didn't have the right to make fun of him. He was a person like them. He deserved respect. He had the right to exist. I told them this man had shown more love and compassion than all of them. I left with him. My friends now taunted me.

We introduced ourselves on the walk to my place. He told me that he had been raised a Christian and he had left the church when he found that they would never accept him, they could never love him. We talked for hours about our lives then and now. How we both came to be in that spot together.

I told him my secret and he told me about a friend of his. She had the same feelings as I. She wasn't gay. She was a transsexual. She had been a man and now was a woman. He told me that I was a transsexual too.

I met his friend, and she explained what it meant to be trans. She told me that I could transition like her. She introduced me to her other friends who were trans. They all had held secrets like mine, and they all had to let them go. They know my secret because it's the same as theirs. They love me just the way I am. They became my family.

I found new work, and I found a new life. I found that God still hadn't answered my prayers, but a surgeon did. God's people know my secret now, and they hate me. I don't hate them. I pity them.

I am happy now. I am myself, and I don't have to hate anyone, including myself.

Why You'll Fight

MAZIKEEN WAGNER

Dear Time-Traveling Past Self,

First of all, the temporal shielding on this trans-dimensional call has been a little wonky, so apologies if we end up triggering a time paradox and wiping out all of space-time. But assuming that doesn't happen...

I am reaching out, because I know just how badly you need a comforting, supportive voice right now. I mean, you talk a big game with your partner and friends, but I know how terrified you are of undertaking this journey of living as the woman you are.

And I see you there, across this vast temporal gap, consumed by the haunting questions until your face goes gaunt. What name should you tell your family and friends to call you by? How will you get the gatekeepers to allow you access to estrogen and spironolactone? Is it even safe to go out in full feminine attire now that you're back in the states far away from the supportive lands of Denmark? Isn't it madness to be out and open in the job you only so recently acquired? What if you never pass because your stocky frame and butch presentation will never be read as a woman's body?

And so, I want to, with arms full of love, reach out and hold you close and whisper in your ear these soft words of support: all your concerns are the wrong damn concerns. Every last fucking one of them.

Well, maybe not all of them. The ones about your world falling out from underneath you were actually damn prophetic. In fact, the next couple of years are going to be even worse than you could possibly imagine.

You will be discriminated out of a job just at the point when you were starting to enjoy being out and accepted as yourself. And while you are reeling from that, you'll be disowned by your previously supportive parents and treated like a confusing and disturbing thing by the uncle who had been like a third parent since before you could form conscious memories. You'll be forced back into a closet, you'll nearly go homeless, and there are going to be times you get way too reminiscent with the blades you used to be intimate with as a child. Your mind will be almost as fragile and fragmented as when you were a wee lass being abandoned by so-called friends who could smell the queerness it would take years for you to see in yourself.

But despite those minor asides (and no matter how much they scar, that's all they'll end up being), all that other shit you were convinced was going to be the most important thing in the world? You'll be shocked how little it will all matter.

'Cause, see, though the toll you will pay breaking down that cold barrier of transphobia by flinging your broken body against it, what you'll actually regret, what will make you slap your forehead to look back at, is all the time you spent deferring to what you imagined the world needed you to be.

To what you convinced yourself would keep you safe and softly placate society's cold ire.

You will waste so much time picking a name that you think will be easier for those you meet to latch onto and accept you with. Not wanting to make people use a silly name stolen from a comic book, you will suffer through so many people using that as an excuse to call you a male name you never had as if to "correct" you on your error. And when you finally say "fuck it," you'll never believe just how successful that name you actually wanted will be. How people will actually compliment you on it and use the correct pronouns.

And let's not dwell on all the time you'll spend slowly trying to ease your family into the concept of transsexuality, being careful not to wear too many skirts or be too frank about your life, worried about pushing them away by throwing them into the deep end too soon... 'Cause a scant few years later that timidness will be used as an excuse to argue that you're delusional and somehow "sprang it on them all of a sudden" years after you came out to them. And it'll turn out the only family member who actually loves and supports you will be the one who accidentally stumbled onto the blog you were radically out on.

Or the worries about "not passing" when it turns out estrogen was just as magical as everyone said it was and will allow you to look in the mirror for the first time without shame and self-revulsion.

'Cause see, the thing about it kid, is despite all the freak outs of those who should have known better, this thing you are doing is as natural as breathing, and it will feel so damn normal it will make you cry.

You will have your partner touch your asexual body or your girlfriend lovingly stare at your naked chest and you'll actually love your body. You will stand in front of a class of suburban Christian homeschool kids in a skirt and a necklace and you will teach them science and no one will even blink.

And you'll finally understand why so many will try to keep you down. Because being yourself is powerful. It feels powerful. It makes you powerful.

You are powerful, my dear past self, so please, I beg of you, stop worrying about what someone will say or if you are being quiet enough to slip by undetected. 'Cause the people who actually matter don't need you to protect them, and those who would demand your silence don't deserve it. So just be yourself. As strongly as you can. You'll thank yourself for it.

I thank you for it.

Mange tak

A Letter to My Sisters

NICOLA COWIE

Dear Sister,

Whatever your journey, and whatever stage of it you are currently at, please try to remember these things. . .

- You are not a freak. It's true we are all unique individuals, each of us different and wonderful in our own ways. It is important however to remember that you are not alone in your uniqueness. There are others in this world who are also on a similar journey, and there is often comfort and healing to be found in community.

- "Comparison is the Thief of Joy" - President Theodore Roosevelt. Try not to judge yourself by the successes and failures of others. It is only all too easy in today's world of perfect bodies and perfect lives being projected at us from all sides by the media, to feel inadequate and a failure. Remember that only by looking back at our own roads can we truly see how far we have come, not by looking at someone else's.

- Just as you are unique, so is everyone else, as is their journey. Despite what the gatekeepers would have you believe, there is no right way or wrong way to transition. There is only the way that is right for you. Others may have a different journey, but that does make it any more or less valid than yours—just different.

- Do not get caught in the web of inaction. You only get one chance at this life. There are no rehearsals, just this live performance. So press forward boldly and strive to claim your happiness.

- Those of us who transitioned later in life did so because of many reasons. Remember, the world was a different place regarding trans women as little as 50 years ago. That is within one lifetime! We each did what we had to do to survive, and each of us transitioned when the time was right for us. Those of us today have benefited from the battles and struggles of those who went before us. They fought often at great cost to forge the paths that we today follow. Similarly we today fight our own battles to forge new paths for those who come after us. The trans kids and youth today have a space, meaning and understanding that we did not. Rejoice in this, because it is a form of legacy that has been forged in our community and carried publicly and proudly by our generation. It doesn't get better by itself, it takes people to make it better, and that is the job of all generations.

- Remember that you did not transition to make others happy. You did it to make yourself happy and complete. If others have problems with what you do, then that is by definition their problem. Very often their issues come from places in their lives that have hurt them. The best way to fight fears and prejudices is with the simple truths of our lives. Live them fearlessly and show the world that you are not ashamed of who we are.

- 3 blessings I wish for you. . .

May you have the insight to know who you are,
the grace to love who you are,
and the strength to be who you are.

I would also like to leave you with a poem I wrote during my transition after an episode of hate speech that was directed at me.

Your Sister,
Nicola Cowie

Words

Words that bite me,
Words that spite me,
Words you throw to mock and slight me.

Words you're jeering,
Words you're sneering,
Words you're sure that I am hearing.

Words deny me,
Words defy me,
Words you use to judge and try me.

Words unheeded,
Words exceeded,
Words my progress unimpeded

Words can't bind me
Words can't find me
Words I choose to leave behind me.

The Gift of Fearlessness

ANDREA JAMES

Dear sister:

It's been decades now, and I'm still in transition.

We're constantly in transition, though most of us rarely think about the many ways we're changing minute by minute. Each day we move through the world, and we hurtle through time. Our experiences change us, and each day is an opportunity to gain new insight and wisdom.

A gender transition is expensive, stressful, and draining, yet you have the ability to reach your goals through realistic expectations and self-acceptance. How many people in the world will ever be able to say they accomplished something that challenging? How many people can say they realized their childhood dreams? You've been given a great gift. Please put it to good use.

If we're open and perceptive to them, we can glean great insights from a gender transition. The greatest insight? Transition can liberate you from fear. As much as we might hope and dream and plan, transition is ultimately a leap of faith, an act of courage. It's never easy, and it's never over. As I write this letter to you, many years have passed since my own transition, and I continue to learn more about myself each day. I never take my good fortune for granted, and I have worked hard to help others have an easier time than I did, because I have been in a position to do so. If you give of yourself without expecting anything in return, your gift will come back to you in all sorts of surprising and unexpected ways.

Many of us have a sense of feeling lost after transition, similar to scaling a difficult mountain, getting to the top, and looking out over the breathtaking vista of everywhere else you could go. As the exhilaration and awe wear off, at some point you must leave that mountaintop in order to get on to the next challenge.

The spectacular view doesn't begin at the top of the mountain. You must find joy in the difficult journey itself, at each step, both up and down. You must look up and around now and then, to marvel at how far you've already come. So many of our sisters will miss the incredible experiences along the way. They get so caught up in the "during" of transition, that they do not marvel at the joys each day can bring. Some even get so exhausted and depleted from the transition process that they don't seek out a new ambitious challenge after transition. That is perhaps the greatest tragedy that can befall you after transition.

My therapist once told me, "There's never a happy ending to an unhappy journey." Don't get so focused on your transition goals and outcome that you defer other dreams.

If you can transition, you can do almost anything else about which you feel that passionately. You have to be very honest about what else you want in life, though. I made the difficult decision to leave graduate school despite getting into the Ph.D. program, because I didn't want to spend my life around the kind of people I'd met in grad school. I got out of advertising because I just did it to make money for transition. Now I create whatever I want and only work with good friends.

What is most important to you? Love? Privacy? Fame? Family? Respect? Health? Solitude? Faith? Stability? Chaos? Only you can answer via deep introspection. Your answer may change over time, too.

The best thing you can do after transition is unplug from the trans scene for a bit and get a fresh perspective. What else do you feel as strongly about as your gender identity? How else would you like to move through the world? What other communities are important to you?

What kind of work would you do if money were not an issue? Then why are you not doing that work? Do what you love and do it well. The money will come, and you will be happier.

How could your social life be different? It's critical to get out of your comfort zone and try new things. It will really help change your focus.

Think about what challenges make you happy in life. If you accept challenges large and small each day and have fun while working on them, there's almost nothing you can't do.

You're already on the path to accomplishing something extraordinary. Now it's time to accomplish something else extraordinary!

I hope this helps, and best of luck!

Take care,
Andrea

Gratitude

"We can only be said to be alive in those moments
when our hearts are conscious of our treasures."
— *Thornton Wilder*

"Gratitude is the sign of noble souls."
— *Aesop*

Remember Why You Started

ARIELLA BASTON

Remember why you started walking towards authenticity, towards a better mirror, towards an existence without incessantly falling into an endless chasm of repression and insufficiency. Remember the choice-less choice to BE WHO YOUR ARE AND WILL YET BECOME.

Even when people attack you, laugh, or use the most hateful words imaginable, remember why you started.

When you're scared of being seen in public, and trying to not to look around yourself to check who might be looking, who might be analyzing, who might be categorizing, who might hit you, remember why you started.

As emotions and impulses explode from a hormone treatment meant to transform your universe exactly as you dreamed and hoped: accept, emote, trust, then return to stillness and remember why you started.

People will leave, but more will arrive to replace them. Trust the refreshing of your resources and support system while you remember why you started.

Recognize the scope of change, which will radiate outward like a supernova from within, and trust that when things look like they're falling apart, they're really just falling into place. You only need to keep radiating that you remember, honor and cherish why you started.

Should you perhaps choose surgery and find yourself clenching your teeth and fists on bed sheets, eyes wet after the 10th hour of holding an ice pack to your body during a marathon of bleeding, remember that you are more than this. You are more than your body and have merely commanded it to catch up to you. It will catch up, healthy and whole, and you'll be able to stop being a patient, to return to being the person you knew to become.

Achievement will happen even when you don't notice. Progress will be made even when all you see is coping. Love will be on a journey towards you, and flowing from you, before you imagine it will. People will appear. Your power will grow, making external validation much more insignificant. You will become fearless and still; content even when taking no action at all. Mundane experiences will become cherished rewards. You'll smile at the mirror and will feel a self-love that will be better than you longed for.

You will see yourself, and finally whisper, "Me. Mine."

All of these will become your ocean of gratitude for why you started, and you'll smile inwardly at how you only needed to start, and then continuously remember why, to find all the strength you need to make it through.

Remember why you started walking towards authenticity, towards a better mirror, towards an existence free of incessantly falling into an endless chasm of repression and insufficiency. Remember the choice-less choice to BE WHO YOUR ARE AND WILL YET BECOME.

The Real Me

LAURA WILSON

It's been a while and some of the thoughts and feelings have faded in my memory. Now, forty years later, it's like you never existed. Still, without you I would not be alive. So I am writing to you now as a way to say "Thanks" and to tell you that your sacrifice was not in vain.

There were never many pictures of you. Not that you were camera shy, you just never liked the way you looked. Photography was only capable of capturing an image that you knew wasn't me. I have fewer of them left now, having had to destroy them for my safety. I still have that one of you at the beach. It was the only one where you smiled and it was easy to tell people that you were my first boyfriend.

It wasn't easy to take those first steps to being me. There were no role models and people weren't very understanding. Still, you found a doctor who would give you estrogen. The first few times you took it were exciting and scary. Your boyfriend at the time didn't understand. "Why would you want to do that, isn't it hard enough being gay?" If being gay was something to hide, being a transsexual was worse. But there was something incomplete about being you. You had the courage to do what was necessary.

It got lonely after that. Your gay friends thought you were going hetero. The heteros thought you were queer. Those early days, you didn't belong anywhere. Although you were never the drag kind of guy, that job as a waitress was a lifesaver. The performers were helpful with your becoming me, teaching you the things you needed to know. It is an experience that you cherish but haven't been able to tell people about.

Those times were lean, but you managed to get a job as a female waitress at a place with better tips. That is where you learned the real nature of sexism. If they only knew, but you didn't dare tell them. At first the other girls thought there was something wrong with you. The lessons from your drag friends worked with the men but not the women. You had to learn how to talk with them. Fortunately, there was Cathy. At first she thought you had been abused, and in a way you had. She helped bring me out and was the first hetero that you revealed yourself to. When she saw the beach picture, she thought it was a shame to waste such a gorgeous guy. People like her were rare and precious.

You managed to save enough money for the surgery. Not long after that there was Michael. At last you had someone who loved you for you. And the sex was life-affirming. But I waited too long to tell him, and he couldn't handle it. Since we'd had the sexual revolution, casual sex was allowed for women. Cathy gave you a t-shirt that said "Good girls go to heaven but bad girls go everywhere!" There were many men, but I was afraid to tell them. This was physically satisfying but emotionally empty. Like my girlfriends, I found some measure of joy with them.

I went back to school and found a better job. This meant better men. Maybe they were just better educated. Then came Karl. He was raised in Europe and a bit more cosmopolitan. I waited, eager to get in the sack but needed to tell him first. That time presented itself and he was OK. He wanted to see and I showed him. I was shaking as I undressed, and there were a million thoughts flashing through my mind. He wanted sex with me! The real me! He stayed, and then he stayed for another twenty-six years. He gave me a good life and he gave me love. That is something that not even the "normals" always get. I got it, and I am grateful.

That's all I wanted to say. To you, the me that was, to Dan for letting me start, to all the performers who raised me, to Cathy for being my sister and to Karl for being my lover and partner. I am grateful, and I am the real me.

Making It

ANONYMOUS
(FROM THE TS ROADMAP)

You may remember me from my earlier letter. I wrote to you about how I nearly overdosed on Vicodin. I was glad that you included the letter on your site.

Today I am writing because I wanted to share with you the great joy that I have found at the end of transition. You see, I made the mistake of thinking that once the surgery was done, the transition was over. How wrong I was! It has been nearly three years since I went under Dr. Meltzer's knife in Portland. But it was only within the last year that I began to feel comfortable in my own skin. Let's fill in some of the gaps...

When I began transition in 1998, I went through all of the legal rigamarole. I jumped through the hoops of the Benjamin Standards with grace and poise. I did the electrolysis. I prepared myself for surgery. But I did not prepare myself for the reception I got at my workplace. And I certainly did not, even with an 18-month RLT, prepare myself for the life I would live after surgery. For me, surgery became an end in itself, rather than a means to an end.

I transitioned "in-place" at my work. I was met with hostility, constant harassment and I was always under threat of termination from my Federal job. But I learned the laws in my home state of California and I used them as a cudgel to beat back management and hold my ground, not to mention my job. I had my surgery on September 5, 2000. Shortly thereafter, I was disowned by my mother, and she passed away only eight months later.

Next, a man that I was very much in love with was murdered by his wife after she found out that we were planning a tryst. I lost all control and relapsed into alcoholism. During my relapse I nearly lost everything: Career, daughter, home. By the time I got sober all I wanted to do was die.

I didn't. Now I am happy to say that while the life I have today is not what I would have chosen, and certainly far from what I had imagined, it is truly beyond my wildest dreams.

I kept my career. I kept my home. I regained the love and respect of my daughter. And I have the most wonderful man in my life who loves me the way I am. I can honestly say that I have walked through the fire and though neither unscathed nor unchanged, I came out more alive than I have ever been in my life. Where I hated the person I was, I can honestly say that I like the person that I am today.

I don't advertise that I am a transsexual woman, but I do not try to conceal the fact either. Most of the people who know me know my story. Those that don't know have no need to know.

I have earned the respect and acceptance of an all-women's Alcoholics Anonymous group. I stand in a room full of women and I am accepted and yes, welcomed. I belong. I finally, really belong to the human race. I finished "rush week" and earned my pledge pin. I have earned my place in the sorority.

For all of our sisters who hesitate and doubt, I would like to go on the record: it can be done. It is not easy and the journey will seemingly demand more from you than you can give, but it can be done.

Dear Jim

JENNIFER FINNEY BOYLAN

Dear James Finney Boylan:

Hey man. How long's it been, fifteen years? How you been? Jeez, you don't look good—don't you moisturize? Here, try some of this. Good stuff, right?

Listen, I know you're afraid right now. Don't be ashamed of that. Fear is a human emotion, and while in future years, people will tell you how brave and courageous they think you are, it's also true that it takes courage to survive the pre-transition time as well. Quite frankly, this condition can peel the bark off of anyone, and I think of you as a hero, you sweet man you. If it weren't for you, you big goofball, I wouldn't even be here. Let's hear it for the boy!

I wish there was something I could say to you that would make it all easier, that would take away the pain, but like a lot of things in life, advice about transition is probably wasted on the people who need it most. You have to stumble through it, making all your mistakes, if you're going to learn anything. It's the mistakes that make us human, not the eluding of them.

Still, here are a few thoughts. I don't know if these will help, but they are the things that come to mind, here in the heart of my middle age.

First, stay off of the television, and keep your name out of print until you are absolutely sure that your story is going to be one worth telling.

I have seen a lot of our sisters rush before the cameras before they were ready, and the result was that yet another trans girl was forever captured in the public eye as vulnerable and uncertain. For a lot of trans women, a television camera can be kind of like The Biggest Mirror in the World. Make sure, if you're going to be on TV, that you're doing it in order to do well by others, and not in order to puff yourself up like Furious Frog. And if you do wind up on TV, remember that you set the agenda. Without you, they don't have a show. So if they try to put you on the defensive, just tell them, Hey. We're not doing that. Make sure you know what your message is going to be, and don't be afraid of practicing it. Before talking to a reporter, memorize the two or three things that you know you want to come out of your mouth. Then, no matter what they ask you, say the things you want to say, regardless of the question.

I know you want to do good in the world, and that doing good, for our people, can mean being public and unashamed. Those are great goals. But, as Bob Dylan says in "Hard Rain's Gonna Fall": 'know your song well before you start singing'.

That also means, if you absolutely insist on being a public spokesperson for trans people, that you understand the full spectrum of what being trans means before starting to hold forth. Your own experience of being trans is only that of one person, and there are lots of ways of doing this. Gender variance comes in lots of different flavors; make sure you understand them all with respect and love before you open your mouth.

If you can, try to stay away from people who would insist that there is only one way to be really trans. The community you are about to join is full of such people, especially on the internet, and if you aren't careful you can wind up in some deranged online argument with a complete stranger eager to tell you that you are "doing it wrong."

But there is no such thing as doing it wrong—only ways of doing it according to someone else's truth, and not your own.

And what is "your own truth," exactly? Well, it may take a while to find out. Be patient. The world can take its sweet time revealing its mysteries to you, and it can be scary to wait years and years for everything to make sense.

I guess the main thing I'd like you to know is that you don't have to be so afraid. The world is more forgiving than you think, and you are a whole lot less important than you believe.

Right now you're pretty obsessed with yourself, with your transition, with the whole strange, ridiculous, miraculous business. Narcissism is kind of your stock in trade. But it can make you kind of unbearable to be around. Try to be open to other people, who have their own triumphs and sorrows, some of them every bit as earth shaking (to them) as being trans is for you.

In the meantime, if you have the chance, try to turn the conversation away from yourself. I know you are very interesting right now, but try to bear this burden with humility. In some ways being so interesting is a little bit like having a disability. You can find a cure, though, by opening your heart to other people. Practice saying the phrase, "But enough about me . . ." You may find that strangers want to pour your hearts out to you right now, and you can do a lot of good in the world by listening.

Anyway, I gotta get back to the 21st century now, but again let me tell you how grateful I am for everything you gave me. I know a lot of trans people who deny their own pasts, who celebrate the dates of their SRS like a second birthday, and I get that. But for us—you and me, Jim—peace has come from seeing our lives as one long continuum, not two stories, but one. It was your courage, and patience, and love that made this life possible.

As we say among my people, "you the man." I love you.

Sincerely,
Jennifer Finney Boylan

Contributor Bios

Calpernia Addams is an ex-Navy Desert Storm combat medic turned Old Hollywood Showgirl. From her earliest beginnings as a child playing bluegrass gospel in an isolated fundamentalist cult deep in the woods of Tennessee, she has experienced a dizzying ascension into her globe-spanning career as a cult-favorite musician, actress and activist for women's and LGBT rights. She has starred in numerous films and television projects, including her own MTV/LOGO television series about dating as a transsexual woman. She has also written a memoir "Mark 947" and composed and arranged countless songs. She has participated in numerous fundraising initiatives and helped raise tremendous sums of money for causes close to her heart. Currently, she lives in Hollywood and tours the world as a cabaret singer, musician and stage performer.

Heather Allen has spent the past few years building a new home and career after leaving a career in the ministry and the only world she knew. She has been a teacher, retail clerk and delivery driver. After transition and a second trip through college, she intends to start a new career in law. She resides in Austin, Texas.

Jillian Atkins is a fifty-three year old woman who transitioned in her early twenties. She is an artist living a private life mostly in stealth. She has a close-knit family and circle of friends who have been the foundation of her creating a happy and healthy life. Since transitioning Jillian has come to feel blessed for the life she has lived and the experiences that have come with her journey.

Ariella Baston is an impassioned Canadian who analyzes all the things for her career in IT. She has also led online communities, counseled people in need, and written self-help content for over a decade. She likes to spend time reading, writing, moonwalking in fuzzy socks, and visiting with friends and family, as well as riding around town in her sky-blue Trek cruiser ("The Diva") in Montreal.

Janis Booth is a native of Connecticut but also lived in California in the 1970s. Now she resides in beautiful downtown Thomaston, Connecticut. Janis has had two full careers. In her first career she worked as a registered nurse in cardiology, emergency medicine, and IV therapy. Now, she is a software developer and currently working at WebMD.

Jenny Boylan is Professor of English and Director of Creative Writing at Colby College. She serves on the Board of Directors of GLAAD, Inc., and the Board of Trustees at the Kinsey Institute for Research in Sex, Gender, and Reproduction. She is the author of 13 books, including *She's Not There* and *Stuck In The Middle With You*. She lives in rural Maine with her partner Deirdre "Grace" Finney, their sons Zach and Sean and a pair of Black Labs.

Zoe Brain was born in the UK and later immigrated to Australia in 1968 at the age of 10. She is literally a rocket scientist. Some of her work is currently orbiting Mercury. She has worked in safety-critical systems engineering, aerospace engineering, missile defense, naval combat and medicine. Currently, she is completing a dissertation on evolutionary computation and lecturing at the Australian National University. She married in 1981 and later transitioned in 2005. She is still married and has one child.

Dianne Chapman lived 26 years as a lost soul until she was finally freed. Those years are now a faded memory. She is a resident of the Boston area with her loving partner of six years. She is an avid fan of the Red Sox and could care less if some people think that's not "girly."

Nicola Cowie is a 50-ish year old woman from the UK. She has been married to her wonderful wife for almost 20 years. Between them they have seven children and six (soon to be seven) grandchildren. In 2008 she finally faced her inner truth and began her transition. The journey towards wholeness and physical congruence between identity and body lasted four years, and also included the international relocations between the USA and the UK. She has worked in the software security industry for over 15 years now and with computers in general for nearly 25 years.

Sally Dellow lives in Upper Hutt, New Zealand. She has worked as an engineering geologist for twenty-five years. She is a parent of two children and is currently living on a 12 acre farm raising cattle and providing living space for the wild animals.

Jenn Dolari has been a comics pusher, cash register slave, Usenet junkie, Mortal Kombat aficionado, video game conceptual artist, tech support guru and web comic publisher. Her comics, "A Wish for Wings" (about a woman's quest to be an angel), and "Closetspace" (about a boy's quest to be a woman) have been wandering around the Internet weekly since 2001. She spends most of her free time in Austin, Texas in a blind panic over how she'll manage to get next week's comics done.

Brigid Fallon is 57 year-old social services veteran. She is living in Oregon with her two cats and two horses.

Carrie Garcia is from Santa Ana, California where she has lived since birth. With the support of a loving family she has been on estrogen since the age of 17. She enjoys spending time with family and friends, working at her mall job, writing poetry, and occasionally attending classes at the community college.

Andrea James is a Los Angeles-based writer, director, producer, and activist focusing on LGBT media and transgender consumer issues. Her work includes consulting on and appearing in *Transamerica* and several other films and television programs, co-producing the first all-transgender *Vagina Monologues* and creating the Transsexual Road Map instructional site

Barbara Kelly is a native of New Jersey but currently resides in Florida with her spouse. Barbara knew at a very young age that her physical body did not match her gender identity. Although brought up in a very religious, conservative family, she fought to live as the woman who she really was and transitioned in the 1970's against all odds. She has gone on to help others in their transition journeys. She has worked in the financial and insurance industries for the past 30 years.

Lara Landis is a freelance writer and blogger. She writes about asexual issues for Examiner.com. She also has a video game habit and delusions of adequacy.

Cheryl Miller was born in Chicago, Illinois but grew up in Los Angeles, California. She is a Navy veteran. She built a successful career in Human Resources and retired in 2010. Since 2004 she has been the moderator for Being ME, a peer support group for MTF transsexuals in Orange County, California. Cheryl enjoys reading, movies, sports, and musicals.

Chelle Munroe is a M/F transgender living full time as a female. She graduated Summa Cum Laude from Boston University with a Bachelor's Degree in Interdisciplinary Studies. Currently, she is retired and pursuing her goals of surgical transition. She is a member of Pink Essence, an online group for transgender people.

Kelly O. is a graduate of Harvard University with doctorates in sociology and psychology. She is happy to have survived the draconian gatekeeper process imposed upon transsexual women. Currently, she advocates for the elimination of pathologizing transwomen and a medically based diagnosis of gender transitioning.

Angela Palermo is a transgender activist, writer, performer, librarian and amateur filmmaker. Her work has appeared in *Trans-Kin, Focus on the Fabulous, Transgender Tapestry* and *Main Street Free Press*. She is considering pursuing an MFA in film and dreams of making a documentary of the Hijras of India.

Shevon Propst was born intersexed and has been living her life as her true self for over 25 years. Although her childhood was filled with abuse from family and classmates, she has learned to hold her head high and thrive. Ms. Propst has spent many years educating the public about transgender issues. She has worked with Arizona State University and other educational facilities as a guest speaker on transgender issues.

Deanne Thornton has spent most of her life in southern California but has travelled to every state in the continental US by van. She has worked as a pastor, teacher, engineer, and software author, as well as owned her own business. Currently, considers herself a recovering theist. When she is not working as a freelance geek, she spends time mentoring and advocating for trans women. She loves movies, reading, cooking/baking, and all things Apple. To this day she still lives with the nagging feeling that her life would have been better if she had only attended Clown College.

Mazikeen Wagner is a science teacher. She is a regular contributor to the blog *Sadly, No!* where she mocks and eviscerates right-wing bigots on a regular basis. She identifies as trans*, poly, and asexual and lives with her partner and cat in standard lesbian stereotype poverty in the San Francisco Bay Area.

Gina White is not sure when her transition began but it was probably in early 2013. In addition to writing prose, she also writes software for a living. Gina loves living in San Francisco where she enjoys sharing time with friends and snuggling with her sweetie. She used to love fishing and wonders when she will get back to that.

Laura Wilson is a caterer, florist and alumni of the University of California, Berkeley. She lives in Decatur, Georgia with two horses and four dogs.

Julie Wong grew up in Honolulu, Hawaii and is a graduate of Stanford University. She transitioned shortly after graduating while living and working in the San Francisco Bay Area. She lives in the Boston area with her two rescue dogs where she enjoys swimming, skiing, and cooking.

DARLIE BREWSTER
COVER ILLUSTRATION AND ARTWORK

Darlie Brewster was born in Canada where she studied animation at Sheridan College. She began work on her first feature film as a senior animator at Rock and Rule in 1981. This book is especially meaningful to her, as it deals with a number of subjects that are close to her heart. Her film credits include *Fern Gully, Hunchback of Notre Dame, The Prince of Egypt, The Road to El Dorado, Horton Hears a Who, Curious George, Asterix* movies, *Family Guy, Road to the Multiverse, Looney Tunes Back in Action, Smurfy Hollow* and *ParaNorman*, to name a few.